NEVER
GIVE UP

To

Connor e Darragh

Best Wishes

NEVER GIVE UP

NIKKI SINCLAIRE

Published in Great Britain 2013 by Junius Press
123 New John Street, Birmingham B6 4LD
www.juniuspress.org

ISBN 978 0 9927442 0 5

A CIP catalogue for this book is available from the British Library.

Typeset by Ian Taylor, Taylor Thorne, Somerset

Printed and bound in Great Britain by
CPI Group (UK) Ltd, Croydon, CR0 4YY

For my Parents and family.
For their love and understanding.

CONTENTS

FOREWORD

They come in all shapes, sizes and colours of the political spectrum. But few politicians of any hue have shown the proven conviction of Member of the European Parliament Nikki Sinclaire.

Since Nikki became an MEP in 2009 she has been a thorn in the side of the European Union and the Government. Her 'divorce' from the UK Independence Party (UKIP) led to an acrimonious split. But Nikki went on to show her determination in 2011, when she and her team raised in excess of 100,000 signatures on a petition, calling for a referendum on the UK's membership of the EU. It pushed the issue to the forefront of the political agenda and onto the floor of the House of Commons. Her aim – somewhat disarmingly – is to make herself and all other MEPs redundant.

I was introduced to Nikki only a couple of years ago through a mutual friend, and have followed her political career with interest. You don't have to agree with her politics to admire her stamina, determination and compassion for her constituents.

Nikki actually puts more than £30,000 a year – audited – of her salary back into her constituency work, making her apparently unique among politicians.

But there were was one great secret that Nikki never shared with anyone other than her close friends and family, and which she writes about here in poignant detail for the first time; Nikki Sinclaire was born a boy.

Hers is a powerful personal story. Yet she insists it is only one facet of her life. Though it tormented her throughout her childhood and teenage years, it is important to her that it does not dominate her future.

Her experience has given her an insatiable urge for justice and she has taken some high profile stands on International Human Rights issues.

As the first 'sex change' Parliamentarian in Britain, Nikki Sinclaire has made history. But she insists she would prefer to be known in the future not as a statistic, but for her heart-felt and conviction politics.

JO KNOWSLEY
London October 2013

INTRODUCTION

I have been involved in politics for almost thirty five years and been a British MEP for four of them.

So why am I telling my extraordinary story – and making such personal, and sometimes painful, revelations – now?

Perhaps it is because I finally feel ready to draw a line under a matter that dominated so much of my young life, often leaving me feeling isolated and tormented. I am now very comfortable in my own skin.

But I also hope that my story, and the many obstacles I overcame, will inspire other people from difficult or underprivileged backgrounds to find a way of realising their dreams, personally and professionally.

The struggle I endured to become the woman I am today has played a critical role in the way I see the world. It has fuelled my hatred of discrimination, and left me with an insatiable desire for fairplay and justice.

I have occasionally been asked questions about my personal life before. I loathed the fact I did not feel free to provide fulsome answers.

Indeed I restricted revealing details of my story to all but a circle of close family and friends.

Was I afraid of ridicule, or that my political views might not subsequently be taken seriously? Perhaps.

However, I also did not want the tag 'the sex change MEP' hanging about my neck like an albatross for my whole political career.

I felt it would haunt, and limit me, as my career developed – perhaps even eroding in the minds of some people – the very serious points I was striving to make.

Today, however, things are very different. I can flag up my political achievements and point to battles hard fought and won – and I hope I can raise the profile of my manifesto for what can and should be done by Britain, regarding the EU, in months and years to come.

I also hope that the chapters at the back of this book might be the first steps, for some people, towards understanding the unwieldy and costly monster that is the European Union, and might even lead some to join my fight for a referendum.

I am not alone in fiercely fighting discrimination. And I am proud of what I have achieved in becoming a woman.

I did not seek election to make personal history, I sought election to stand up for the silent majority, those whose voices are ignored by the usual, professional, arrogant political class.

It is my political achievements, not my personal struggles, for which I hope, at the end of it all, to be recognised and remembered.

1 | ANATOMY OF A BODY

Rain teemed on the great glass walls of the European Parliament building in Brussels; it was two o'clock on a winter's afternoon in 2011, but already so dark that all the lights had been turned on. A perfect moment, then, to go exploring. I left my office and set off down the corridors of power.

'I may be some time,' I told my bemused assistant.

I'd had a tip-off. In 2005, a year after the horrific Madrid commuter train bombings and around the time of a very similar attack in London, the EU parliament had spent a lot of money on improved security at its buildings in Brussels and Strasbourg. A lot of money in EU terms really is a lot: in the stuff pours, out it goes, all without audit. And on this occasion, half a million pounds had been spent on the approved purchase of six body-scanners. They were the most advanced type and had been waved through, presumably, among a long list of other items.

Only when the things were on site and scheduled for installation did MEPs belatedly realise that advanced body scanners show you naked. What? Members of the European Parliament? Not likely. Dignity must be preserved. It was an invasion of privacy. An affront to civil liberty.

The scanners disappeared. They hadn't even been unpacked. Presumably their return to the maker had been negotiated. At a discount? No. Perhaps they'd been sold for dismantling and recycling? No. Advertised on e-bay? No. Put up for sale on a card in a newsagent's window? Apparently not.

I'd been told they were still in the building – in store, unwanted and probably unsaleable in Europe as they were no longer at snooping's cutting edge. Was this true? If so it was an example of careless

1

squandering of taxpayers' money, and I believed the taxpayers who had forked out for them should know.

In the lift, on my way down to the basement, people got in and out. But as we sank below the ground floor level I was the only person still inside. Alone, I stepped out into a low-ceilinged windowless corridor, accompanied by a persistent if barely audible hiss from its ventilation system, and started walking.

I was reminded of a famous old mad-house in Vienna called the Narrenturm. It's circular. Every floor is the same. The corridors seemingly endless.

After twenty minutes aimlessly searching, I found myself back at the starting point. I began to orientate myself better after that.

I hunted for those scanners for two hours. I had an access-all-areas pass, so I just kept going, peering into stores, delving into racks of shelving. I passed people in overalls with cardboard boxes, people in smart suits scanning bits of paper, and even a couple of MEPs looking cagey and trying to get a phone signal. But I didn't pass anything that looked eight feet high and about three feet wide.

Until I turned a corner, and there, in the next corridor, upright on pallets on the ground, stood a row of enormous airport-style scanners, four of them already unpacked.

They were stacked beside some stairs. I ran up two flights, found my way back to my office, fetched my assistant and together we returned to the basement. He took my photograph alongside the redundant scanners and an article revealing the ludicrous waste of money appeared later that week in The Sunday Times.

As a euro-sceptic MEP I'm well known for disliking the corruption, hypocrisy and incompetence that are systemic in the European Union. The institution I work in is its Parliament, so I cheerfully disseminate information about life as I see it all around me. MEPs can sign in and immediately leave, having collected €304 with no questions asked. The

Commissioner, who is pleased to impose stringent regulations as to energy consumption, doesn't appear to mind when lights are left on all night in the empty Commission building. MEPs can claim for hair removal, face-lifts and nose jobs at taxpayers' expense. They take trips to 'better understand the fishing industry' in the Seychelles. Oh, and the winemakers of Portugal received an investigative visit much enjoyed by all.

As I write MEPs are demanding the use of full body scanners in airports across the EU. Where is the competence here? This is a federalising project, but we have all grown up apart and don't share the same sense of what it is to be a European.

All this is petty by comparison with the constipation of the whole system and the profligate use of our money. I mind as much as I do because I identify with the disadvantaged. I've been a poor child: rich in having a big family behind me, but not brought up to be socially or culturally advantaged. I want a country that can afford a good health service and good education for all. Most of all I think democracy matters, which means, as somebody pointed out in the middle of the nineteenth century, educating our masters, the voters.

Stop an English person in the street, and they may vaguely know who the Prime Minister is and maybe even the Leader of the Opposition. Too few know how Government works Parliament is the legislature (that passes laws), the Civil Service advises the executive branch (the Prime Misister and the Cabinet). The Judiciary, the judges who administer the law, are independent.

Most people know very little about the European Union, where 75% of our laws originate. We were taken into it without a vote, so why would we? I go into schools and have to explain the difference between the EU Parliament, the EU Commission and the Council. If schoolchildren have no idea who is appointed, who is elected, and how this affects their own lives, you can be sure that their parents don't.

Initiating any piece of legislation can take years, with the competing interest of 28 countries (29 if Serbia joins, with others waiting in the wings). Poles, for instance, probably would not want a ban on alcohol that's more than 40% proof. The French and Italians don't want anyone reducing their profits from agriculture and we Brits value our position in global finance too highly to see it weakened.

The Commission is unwieldy. It employs tens of thousands of people, mostly in buildings all over Brussels, but with a sizeable outpost in Luxembourg, representative offices in every EU country, specialist institutions in several, and more than hundred delegations and specialist officers located all over the world.

Among its duties is the enforcement of EU regulations, necessitating an Inspectorate capable of calling Governments to account.

But it doesn't have one. EU Directives are up to each country to administer and police. It was the Food Safety Authority of Ireland (FSAI), for instance, which first uncovered the EU-wide horsemeat scandal.

As an MEP, I get dozens of letters from people who are in personal difficulty. My hardworking team and I can very often help. But when anything clashes with EU law, I often can't. Much of the mail in my postbag comes from people concerned about animal welfare. (If you are unsure of what a battery hen's predicament might be, look at the Compassion in World Farming website.)

The EU has rules. Campaigners in Britain are delighted that EU law has been implemented and the cruel, tiny, battery cages outlawed for good. The Department for Food and Rural Affairs (DEFRA) has implemented it, and inspectors have verified that British chicken farmers are no longer using these cramped cages.

Yet you can still buy ridiculously cheap egg products at all supermarkets, which have come in from Poland and other EU countries where welfare standards are either evaded, or not policed at all. The EU has no effective powers of enforcement. We could sign up to every EU law, allow flagrant transgressions of the law, be tried and fined millions a day, but if we chose to continue breaking the law – either paying our fine as if it were a tax, or never paying it at all – there's nothing the EU can do. Most of the time, the EU doesn't even try to enforce its own regulations.

It is if our own government had a Parliament, and Civil Service, but no police force or Serious Fraud Office, no Inspectors of Taxes, and no bailiffs to enforce non-payment of fines. The EU Court of Justice – the EU's judiciary arm – can impose fines on a whole country, but if that country decides not to pay them the Court is powerless to act. For three years until 2002, the French Government would not allow the import of British beef. The EU Court of Justice had ruled this was in restraint of trade, and fined them £250,000 a day for as long as the stance continued. France neither paid up, nor changed its ways. Eventually it allowed imports to restart. But France never paid that fine and never will.

Is it any wonder that a woman who started out life in a cramped council estate, at the heart of a working class family, and began work as a junior accounts clerk in Croydon gets so indignant? My knowledge and sense of justice were slowly and painfully acquired. Now I want everybody to be given as much information as they want and need. It's good for you. It's empowering. Perhaps for me, in particular, as for much of my early life I felt like an outsider.

For not only have I battled prejudice, and poverty. I was born a boy.

2 | WHO AM I?

I was born opposite the Houses of Parliament, at St Thomas' Hospital on Friday 26 July, 1968, at 1pm – the same time and day of the week that my dad received his pay, which he never lets me forget.

I grew up a Brixton kid, surrounded by people: my younger brother and two younger sisters, cousins, playmates off the estate and my Irish nanna, who'd come to London as a widow with her tribe of daughters in the early sixties. I learned the Rosary with my nanna and my mum in the kitchen of our two bedroom flat. My dad was a lorry driver and my mum, when she worked outside the home, did cleaning, or worked as a canteen assistant.

When I was only four, to give my mum a bit of peace and quiet when she had two toddlers and a baby in a two-bedroomed flat, and was pregnant again, my dad used to take me out in his lorry. I seemed to go out with him almost every day, sitting alongside him in the passenger seat of the cab with a pile of jam sandwiches on my lap. He was a big man, six foot two and strong, and he would deliver goods all over London.

I absolutely loved it: the North London terraces, Battersea Park, whole streets of creamy stucco houses in Kensington, Streatham High Road with the big old mansion blocks and the cinema, Waterloo Bridge, St Paul's, Nelson's Column – every day was different and so were the people. It was like watching an endlessly entertaining film.

It taught me that my little world wasn't the only one. Too many kids never learn this. I wanted to drive all over the city too.

Being at home in Brixton, with my mum, was magical too. We lived just round the corner from the tube, the Town Hall and our Catholic Church. I loved the crowds on the streets, delicious-smelling jerk chicken, Indian spices in the market, buses and pubs, fire engines, the sounds of reggae music drifting from the neighbours' windows, gospel singing from the church across the road – the colour of it all.

Mum took me on the bus sometimes to see an aunty. When we went past a church she'd bless herself. I was an observant child, and once noticed she hadn't crossed herself as we passed a church.

'Why don't you cross yourself Mum? That's a church there.'

She answered in an undertone. 'It's Proddy. It's different.' 'How different?' I asked. 'They don't believe in Our Lady,' she countered, answering my question about whether we could go in with a firm: 'No! It's a mortal sin. Now ssh.'

Everything was almost perfect in my little world. But not completely; something about myself made me uneasy – though at first I had no idea what it was.

I remember listening to my nanna, aunties and mother as they sat around the kitchen table, drinking tea and putting the world to rights.

A faint miasma of seriousness and concealment surrounded these conversations. They were big pow-wows, mysteries being discussed and decisions being made by the women at the centre of power. I knew from around the age of three or four that I didn't feel comfortable with being a boy. I just felt wrong, uncomfortable about who I was. But I couldn't say 'Mum, there's something wrong.' I knew I was a girl in the wrong body, but instinctively, I knew I couldn't tell anyone.

In my night prayers, I would pray to Our Lady, God, Jesus, St Anthony that I would wake up a girl. I could never understand why my prayers were not answered, I was good.

Then, when I was five, I began having the same dream almost every night. In the dream I would wake up as a girl and everything would be alright. Then I really woke up and I was still a boy. It is at this time it began to be painful. The ache was emanating from the middle of my body, or was it my soul? I was confused.

On my first day of school we were allowed into the playground in the afternoon and I headed straight for the Wendy House, where I dressed up in all the girls' clothing that was there and played happily with the girls and the dolls. I also liked drawing little pictures of houses. This was repeated on a daily basis.

The teachers obviously didn't think it important enough to inform my parents, otherwise I'm sure my dad would have had something to say.

Things were not right. But what options were there? Better to shut it all off and try not to worry about it.

By the time I was seven we were living in Carshalton near Croydon. We'd had to leave Brixton three years before, because the flat was officially too small for us and we couldn't get rehoused anywhere except a dull new town that I prefer to forget, but where I'd started school and made my first Communion. The wafer stuck to the roof of my mouth.

I didn't like school. It was a Catholic school, but it wasn't warm and inclusive like home. I liked reading, but I didn't get on with the teachers and couldn't relate to the other boys. I looked as if I fitted in. Dad had insisted that I should have the right uniform, the cap and the miniature blazer and tie.

After about a year we came back to London, to Blackheath, where mum and dad ran a fish and chip shop. Dad had a Vauxhall Cresta and I'd sit behind the steering wheel, imagining driving myself around the 'world', which for me was London. To this day I love driving, have my most creative thoughts there and I own a 1967 Wolsley which I think takes me back to that period.

We were happy in Blackheath, but then some other mysterious problem occurred and we ended up moving – carting all our stuff from flat to flat several times.

When the poor move, there is no question of tea-chests, packers and a removal van with men in overalls. The poor do it with cardboard boxes, old travel bags and anything else that'll do as a receptacle including buckets and washing-up bowls; everybody moves along with the stuff, including the telly, in whatever sorry motorised vehicle you can get.

At one point we ended up in emergency accommodation – one squalid room for the six of us and whatever stuff we had left. The council estate was certainly not in a posh part of Carshalton, but it was isolated, rough, bleak and a bit intimidating.

The whole estate was only about ten years old. It was a dead-flat stretch of land with about a dozen low-rise blocks and wide patches of scrubby grass where you could kick a ball about or walk a dog. The depressing 'facilities' included a grubby launderette and playground.

The blocks were long and four storeys high and the accommodation consisted of maisonettes, one on top of the other. Imagine a row of boxy two-storey terraced houses, each with its own garden, surmounted by an identical row on top – only instead of gardens, the ones on top shared a long walled balcony. We'd moved into one of the upper maisonettes. Dad was on the lorries again so there was money coming in.

And we had a car of our own, a beautiful elderly Daimler Mark II. A Daimler Jag it was called. Dad spent hours with his head under the bonnet and oil cans and spanners all over the tarmac. If I climbed on a chair I could see him from our bedroom window, along with my brother hanging around watching and helping. My brother and I were close although we were very different. I liked stories; he liked engines.

But then something unimaginable happened. It was a Bank Holiday: Easter Monday, 1976. The family had been out in the car on a lovely sunny day. When we got back, mum and dad went indoors while I went to the playground with my siblings.

For some reason, I felt the need to go home. As I turned the corner,

I could see my dad and one of the neighbours, a big fellow like him, up on the balcony. Dad had his white shirt sleeves rolled up and was close to the balcony wall. The neighbour made a sudden movement and I watched dad flying over the edge.

Twenty feet up. On his back in a strange, mid-air sprawl.

I ran. I had to catch him.

I was stopped only by a shut gate into a front garden. Dad landed with a bang. I knew if the gate hadn't been there I'd have caught him. Dad lay there lying slightly on one side, motionless, barely conscious, sun reflecting off the white shirt.

The neighbour lived three doors down along the balcony. There had been some dispute with my father. I don't know what it was. He'd tipped dad over the edge then walked back along the balcony casually peering over. I shrieked as I looked up. He was smiling. I thought my dad was dying.

'Get help,' he whispered. 'Get help.'

I tore up the stairwell screaming and ran into a man. He couldn't understand a word I said. I was calling my mum and trying to explain to the man what had happened. Upstairs my mum didn't answer and by the time I got back outside there were other people congregating.

The man's wife went into our maisonette and told my mum what her husband had done. My mum rushed to the scene distraught. An ambulance came and the men started moving dad onto a stretcher to take him to St. Helier Hospital. By this time my brother and sisters had been brought from the playground. My brother looked stricken. He was only five. A woman said to my mum 'We'll take your kids for you, you go with him love.'

I felt as if my insides had just caved in.

My sisters didn't properly understand it. They just went back to the playground and carried on messing about. My brother and I went with them but I knew something really bad had happened. I don't remember much else about that afternoon except all of us kids being in the neighbours' house, and my uncles, from my dad's side, being there. He had six brothers and some of them had driven over from North London. They talked to the grown-ups mostly, and told us to behave ourselves.

The police came and arrested the neighbour, took him away, and released him on police bail the following morning.

Very late on that first night my mum told me: 'Your dad's all right, but he's not very well.' My dad was just 32.

What she didn't tell us was that the doctors had said he would never walk again. But kids pick up a lot from listening to the grown-ups and I knew.

My grandmother, my dad's mother up in Harrow in North London, telephoned the following morning and said: 'I'll take two of them.' She wanted to look after the oldest and quietest children, which was me, and my baby sister who was about two. My mum said: 'No. They're going to stay here.'

There was dark disapproval in that relationship. Our mum thought her mother-in-law was stuck up and wouldn't take the middle children because they had bright red hair which made them look Irish. My dad's dad was of Irish descent, but he'd left our grandmother years ago. She was from Harrow and proud of it. Harrow was not London, and that mattered to her. She had married up, four times. We didn't know her well and when we went over there we had to dress in our best and mind our Ps and Qs.

Mum's own mother, our Irish nanna from Brixton, who we knew well and who'd helped to teach me my catechism, came over for the first few days and went on doing so, back and forth, all summer.

Easter was only just over. It had meant several trips to church for Mass, and long services. I felt very serious, all of a sudden, about praying. But dad was still sick and nothing good was happening.

Boys are usually slow developers. But I wasn't. I volunteered to be an altar server, wearing a neat surplice, following the service, standing, sitting and kneeling at all the right times, carrying the cross or candle and passing the wafers and chalice to the priest at Communion. I soon knew all the words by heart. I had internalised all the teachings long ago: the significance of the Eucharist that we Catholics believe is the body of Christ, and that sin was wrong and Jesus was watching over you, and that if you did anything wrong the Virgin Mary would cry. I believed all of it; why wouldn't I? I had learned it from my mother and my grandmother.

We were taken to see dad in hospital. One leg was in a caliper and he was still barely conscious, I suppose heavily anaesthetised. His pelvis was completely smashed up. He had probably only survived because he was so physically strong: a lorry driver used to hauling stuff around. They lifted and carried everything then.

I felt an enormous sense of responsibility for my brother and sisters. It was overwhelming; enough to temporarily sweep aside my concerns about the gender issue.

Dad was in hospital for months. The car was sold. My mum had to be on social security. She was desperate for us to get rehoused somewhere else because the criminal neighbour had been released the day after it happened and was still living in his masionette along the balcony. Statements had been taken and at some point – I'm not sure when – he was charged with Grievous Bodily Harm and listed for trial at the Old Bailey.

In the meantime, we were running into him on the stairs. I often saw him. Once our mum had some argument with his wife and I heard the woman snarl 'If you don't shut up we'll put you over the balcony same as we did to your old man.'

We went back to school, but by then I was used to going to St Helier Hospital to visit, so I went to see dad every day. If I had fourpence I got the bus after school, or sometimes I walked. Once or twice when I got tired (it was already hot in June that year) I would phone 999 and say I was lost and get the police to give me a lift home in their noddy car.

The local authority would not rehouse us because there were some rent arrears. Everything seemed so difficult; the social security money went nowhere. I got a few coins for helping at christenings and other church services – never for being an altar server, you did that for free, but at christenings and weddings you'd often get a tip. I washed cars as well. I was grimly conscious of my mum's struggle and gave the money to her straight away, although usually I would go and buy milk or Weetabix with it before I got home. It was comforting to earn money and see it put to good use. It helped me to feel we'd get through this.

My childhood had ended when I saw dad falling. When I hear of people lifting cars off other people in an emergency, I never doubt that shock can give you a burst of almost superhuman power. It's fortunate that the garden gate stopped me when I saw Dad fall, because I still half-believe I might have caught him, and died in the attempt.

In July I would be eight, yet already I felt I'd taken on a burden, and more was to come. A couple of weeks before my birthday, I woke up to find my mum was in terrible pain. I called an ambulance. It turned out she had gallstones and would have to stay in hospital for an operation.

A couple of women from social services came round. We were four children under eight, and they wanted us taken into care. My dad had told us all about that. He'd been in care and in institutions from a very early age, and he'd told us how he got beaten, about cruel nuns and a horrible boarding school he'd gone to. I was terrified. I phoned one of my aunts, while the social security people were in the sitting room and begged her to stop social services from taking us.

In the end, we were allowed to all stay with her in Essex. I didn't see my dad for the next four weeks, but the four of us were together, and we were safe with my auntie. My mum was in hospital for two weeks and then she had two weeks' convalescence. We went back home after that, and I saw my dad in hospital over the rest of that boiling summer.

When he came home in September, it was to the same maisonette, with the perpetrator and his wife still three doors down. We all stood at the door as dad emerged from the ambulance in a wheelchair. One leg was just wasted by inactivity, but the other stuck straight out in a huge leather and steel caliper from hip to ankle.

There was no lift. The ambulance people got him upstairs somehow. That night, my mum and I had to get the caliper off and help him to heave himself out of the chair and into the bed. In the morning, we had to do the same again in reverse. The caliper had loads of straps; you couldn't leave a single one untightened, because they all had to support bone and sinew and keep the whole pinned-up limb together.

A physiotherapist was sent out to see him, and since dad was determined and fit, he arranged an ambulance to take him to some sort of centre once a week where he could practice getting out of the wheelchair and standing. He kept saying he was going to walk, he was going to drive. 'And it won't be a disabled car. I'll get back to work again.' His identity was bound up with being a lorry driver, a working man, proud of his skill.

Inflation was soaring. In the autumn my mum had to scrape extra money together to buy Dad a new pair of shoes. One set of caliper straps went under his foot, and since he kept trying to stand and take a few steps, the physiotherapist told her that his shoes must be brand new because any wear on the soles would put his gait out of balance.

I was helping mum get him out of bed in the mornings, going to school and coming home to find dad watching TV on the sofa. I'd sit and watch it with him. Especially the news at 5.45 at night. There was social unrest at the time and he'd explain things to me; about rich people and how working people had always had to fight to get paid enough.

My mum went out cleaning. The Local Authority gave out vouchers to buy some of the school uniform and we got free school dinners. It was a Catholic school and the priest came and helped with some money. One day I was told we'd be playing football and I hadn't got any boots, so I was given an old pair of regular shoes to wear. Other kids looked down on you for these things. My brother was only eighteen months younger but, because of his month of birth, two years behind me at school. He would always react fiercely to aggression, but I'd just walk off when kids got spiteful.

I didn't like school and never had, and by now I'd been to quite a few. I didn't fit in and I thought it was a waste of time. I didn't like the teachers or want to play with other boys. I liked reading, and I used to get books out of the school library – Ladybird ones, with big print on one page and colourful pictures opposite, were my favourite. I devoured Kings and Queens of England, Part One, and spent ages looking for Part Two before I found it. Elizabeth I and Queen Victoria were the figures I most admired: proud of their country, opinionated, determined, and of course, women. I wanted to be like them. There had been a dramatised biography about Edward VII, Queen Victoria's son, on television. I was riveted. My brother wasn't interested.

I read all the Catholic stories too. I loved going to church: the incense, the ritual, and the security you got from feeling that there was a plan and God was in charge of it. I would make my confession regularly ('I was rude to my mum' got you five Hail Mary's) and take communion. I told my mum I was going to be a priest.

I thought it would please my mother and my nanna. Although I felt like a girl I didn't know I was ever going to be able to become one. I think I thought that by becoming a priest it might be a way to disguise my problem. My mother was pleased, but dad didn't say anything. He was not religious. A priest would not be unacceptable in our family, but seemed wildly unlikely.

Winter was coming and the days grew shorter. Dad used to tell us that the neighbour was going to the Old Bailey soon and would be sent to prison, and we'd get compensation.

'Then we'll have a nice house with a swing in the garden.'

'And a decent set of curtains,' my mum would say.

'Lovely lovely curtains. And a big fridge full of ice cream.'

None of it ever materialised. The neighbour was acquitted so we got nothing from the Criminal Injuries Compensation Board. He stood in the dock and claimed he'd acted in self-defence; my dad had swung a punch at him, missed, and gone over the balcony. The jury believed him. I was certain, because I had been watching at the time, that his version of events was a lie, but I was too young to testify and there were no other witnesses. The accused's wife cannot be made to give evidence against him, and anything my mother might have said was hearsay.

My sense of injustice was coruscating. We were all powerless. There seemed to be no further action we could take.

But in '77 things started looking up. After Christmas we were finally offered an old inter-war house, quite big, in South Croydon. Dad was already on crutches. My mum got another cleaning job and took over as the main breadwinner until my dad could get work. Gradually, week by week, he became more nimble. One crutch was discarded, then the other. I learned a lot from him: grit, persistence. Never giving up.

He was lame, but when spring came, he'd started to drive again. That summer, the summer of the Queen's Silver Jubilee, he got a job back on the lorries.

3 | THE BEST THING EVER

Ours wasn't a political household in the sophisticated sense, but my fad had strong views that he expressed with some force for the benefit of ITN newsreader Alastair Burnet and me. I was usually hanging over the back of the sofa and would hear his gruff tones mutter 'Expletive Expletive Government.'

Later, when we were driving, dad beeped the horn in support of the striking firemen – we had a fire station near where we lived, and they used to huddle round a brazier outside. That was late 1978, the Winter of Discontent, when you'd see Green Goddesses – thumping great military vehicles equipped for firefighting – rolling down the streets. Jim Callaghan, the Labour Prime Minister, was on TV, saying that he wasn't going to call a General Election but would carry on governing.

I was ten. How all this joined up was unclear to me. I knew the faces of Callaghan and Margaret Thatcher. I had heard that Russians were our enemies. It was the TUC and the IMF that I didn't understand. And of course I was still a boy.

We'd moved to an estate in New Addington outside Croydon. As the winter progressed and I kept watching the news something else began to puzzle me. According to my dad, the unions and the Labour party supported the working man. But the Labour party was fighting the unions, which were trying to get more money for the working man. There were strikes. When I was sent out to the shops I had to queue for bread. I saw black bags of rubbish piled high on the streets. On TV they said morgues in Liverpool were full of corpses that hadn't been buried.

How could the unions, which represented the working class, be at war with the Labour party? I never got a satisfactory answer.

19

Events were moving fast. Jim Callaghan suffered a vote of No Confidence and he came on TV to announce that there was going to be a General Election. In 1979, Prime Ministers did not Tweet. They sat at a desk in Number Ten and spoke directly into camera with their eyes sliding inexpertly along the autocue. I watched Jim Callaghan. I knew that an Election was coming after all and was immensely pleased. I was already fascinated by politics, though I had no notion I could ever become a politician.

If you followed the news every day as I did, it was exciting. Like a race. I already admired Margaret Thatcher. She reminded me of the first Queen Elizabeth: brave, forthright, independent-minded – and the Russians, our enemies, called her the Iron Lady. She sounded posh, but she talked about the hardships working people were having and how they should be free to own houses and start businesses and how her dad had been a grocer. I thought it was all brilliant. I got keener and keener.

Dad brought the Evening Standard home. Also he sometimes got the Sun, originally a left-leaning paper for the working man, but now distinctly of the right. I read these and the News of the World, which my Dad bought every Sunday, and I grew some political understanding. I debated the points with my Dad but he still couldn't explain how, as a Labour supporter, he could also support the strikers.

When he had no answer I made it my business to personally rally support for Margaret Thatcher. I went out in the Easter holidays rapping on doors with a sense of importance. Blokes in shirt-sleeves and braces would open the front door and look down to see a skinny ten-year-old. 'Hallo,' I squeaked. 'I don't know if you know about the General Election but I think you should vote for Margaret Thatcher.' Jaws dropped. Then they smirked. 'Not bloody likely.' I was entirely serious. I moved on to the next front door, undeterred.

When she won, and appeared in a blaze of flashbulbs outside Downing Street and quoted St Francis of Assisi, I was bursting with pride. Dad sat quietly abusing the screen. 'Where there is discord, may we bring harmony,' intoned Mrs T. 'Where there is error, may we bring truth. Where there is doubt, may we bring faith…and where there is despair, may we bring hope.' He looked as if he'd sucked every last bit of juice from a lemon.

It sounded pretty promising to me. I knew the Houses of Parliament, Downing Street and Buckingham Palace from having gone past in the car; and we'd been to a Remembrance Day service in Whitehall. This huge drama was being enacted in a place I'd been to. I could be there.

I'd attended about ten schools by now, and had been disruptive in all of them. I was not friendly with many other boys and I was uninterested in anything except History, Geography, Religious Education and football. Reports were scathing. I exhibited what's now called 'challenging behaviour' ('mouthy little sod'). But the CofE school where I spent my last term at a primary took us on a day trip to France, on a Hovercraft. I was the first member of my family who'd ever gone outside Ireland or the United Kingdom and I thought it was wonderful. I devoured a book called 'Living in America', and then took all the others in the series out of the library one by one: 'Living in China', 'Living in Australia', 'Living in France' – I thought WOW! I wanted to travel to all of these places and live in all of them. I wanted to learn French.

Life seemed full of mismatches. Family and school were different worlds, my schoolwork and my aspirations bore no relation to each other, and as for being a boy, that was off the scale. I was nearly eleven, it was 1981, and every day I still woke up having dreamed about being a girl and being able to do anything, without obstruction. The disappointment was harsh, I buried my face into the pillow and cried. The rational part of me believed this could never happen. But I didn't confront that. I suppose I compartmentalised. You learn to do that, as a Catholic. If you admit scientific fact, and lose your religion, what do you have?

At the same time Britain was engulfed in a climate of fear. It was the height of concerns about a nuclear attack and the Government put out a public leaflet, dropped through the door of every home, that detailed what to do in the event of a nuclear bomb and fallout. Horrors like this overtook my own problems, and concerns about my gender.

At this time there was no 11-plus exam, but still it wouldn't be easy to get into a good secondary school. I did well in tests, except for Maths, but my behaviour got me bad reviews. I'd told my class teacher I wanted to be a priest and he'd let out a snort of laughter, so when he heard that summer that I'd got into the best Catholic school in Croydon, he was thunderstruck. Everyone in the staff-room shook their heads in disbelief. I'd walked it at the interview. It was an old, dignified school at the bustling centre of town, very formal and quiet, and I'd had to impress a collection of priests. I was always attentive in church, fervent in my beliefs and solidly grounded in the Catechism. A boy so obviously, enthusiastically devout probably came before them once in a generation and they were delighted.

We got a lodger that summer, an older cousin. He'd been to Borstal and was barred from every pub in Brixton. The last time he went to court, he was released with a probation order on condition that he'd get himself a job and live somewhere else, namely, with us, in safe suburbia. I was used to thinking of myself as top dog, after mum and dad, and because he was older the family dynamic changed. At first, I resented him, but I ended up being glad he was there.

At the Church of England primary the other kids knew I was different because I had to have a priest come in for special classes. I made friends, as usual, with the girls. I did netball and French skipping. Bullies singled me out. Inside I fantasised about living as a normal little girl. I was older in my outlook than other boys. And the cousin distracted me with stamp-collecting. My Harrow granny had given me a big bag of stamps, little sticky mounts, and an album for Christmas. Exotic stamps with things like Magyar Posta and Helvetica written on them. They had pictures and maps and historical events and if my cousin couldn't answer my questions I could look up the information in the encyclopaedia at school. He'd collected British mint stamps at my age and he got me to see how interesting they were. I went out and bought a First Day Cover myself – a set issued to celebrate first European elections.

The cousin did well when he was with us. He behaved himself beautifully, found work in the Coca- Cola bottling plant in South Croydon, got spruced up, saved money and eventually got a place of his own. Then one night he got his pay packet, went into Brixton for a drink with his mates – and having broken the terms of his probation managed to get drunk, become disorderly and get arrested. He was sent down and we didn't see him again.

I couldn't take up the place at the excellent Catholic school that September after all. It was something to do with our move to Thamesmead, which might or might not happen, and the cost of the uniform. I had to go to another Catholic school – less prestigious and co-ed, rather than single sex – in a suburb of Croydon,

From day one, it was awful. Classes were mixed but the playgrounds were segregated: boys in one, girls in the other. If you know inside that you are a girl in the wrong body and you're sent to a place full of eleven-year-old boys whose testosterone levels are just starting to boil you get mashed, and I did. In the first term I had a front tooth knocked out.

This turned out to be the best thing ever.

4 | CROSSING THE RIVER

My dad was furious. What had the effing teachers been doing? Nobody answered. My mouth was a mess and I would need years of orthodontic treatment at King's College Hospital, in Camberwell. A boy's jawline can change dramatically around puberty and they wanted to be sure that no malocclusion developed. As I grew, the orthodontists would have to realign my teeth with a series of braces and check my progress every six weeks.

At first the appointments were even closer together. I would come out of school at lunchtime, meet my mum and we'd set off on the 109 bus from Croydon through Thornton Heath, Streatham and Brixton; a journey we'd made loads of times to visit the aunties and my grandmother. Then we'd change buses for the last few miles to Denmark Hill where the hospital was. The whole ride took more than an hour, and you had to wait before you were seen, so the day was gone.

So after a couple of times, I told my mum I would go by myself. She was relieved. I went off in the morning to catch the bus to school. The appointments were usually in the afternoon; I was supposed to leave school after lunch. That morning, when the other kids got off the bus to go to school, I wasn't with them.

I stayed on the bus as it journeyed through Thornton Heath, Streatham, Brixton, Oval, Westminster Bridge, Parliament Square, and Whitehall, getting off at Trafalgar Square. That first day, I just walked around until it was time to get another bus to the hospital. I trawled the back streets of Covent Garden, quiet in the daytime with stacked-up market boxes everywhere; Leicester Square, scruffy, friendly and a bit sinister; Pall Mall, where uniformed doormen raised an arm and taxis stopped for well-off people to get in. I saw flashes of body language I only half understood and conversations I only half heard; I saw slinky, sultry kids with dyed hair from St Martin's, not much older than me; and heard the buzz of foreign languages. By crossing the river, I'd found a different world. I loved it.

What I loved most was being ignored. In my school blazer I easily melted into the general mix of tourists, shoppers, street sweepers, office workers, shop assistants, hotel staff, students, beggars, photographers – everybody went about their business and nobody noticed me. It was exciting because it proved that I could be as independent as I wanted to be and nobody would stop me.

I knew that if I was ever going to grow into the identity that I vaguely wanted to find, I would have to do it alone. I didn't have the words to express this as a drive to self-realisation, but that's what it was, and I instinctively knew that if I stuck to the options expected of me – lorry driver, factory worker, priest – I would never get anywhere. A Roman Catholic priest has to be a man. I now knew that this would not be right for me. I had begun to understand my inner conflict and knew, somehow, I had to find a way to be my true self – though at this time I had no answers.

London buses were my outlet, my release of tension, my private time when I could live entirely in the present. Imaginary future lives unfolded as I sat on the top deck, devouring the street scene. Soon I was bunking off school a day a week and reappearing the following school day with a note signed by 'my mum'. I cleaned cars for pocket money and the fares were nothing, because bus rides were my lifeline. I started going into the National Gallery and especially the National Portrait Gallery, where I spent hours looking at pictures of Kings and Queens, writers and artists and famous scientists. I was especially fascinated by the clothes in the old portraits.

Nobody, on the buses or streets or in the public buildings, ever asked me what I was doing. If they had I would have told them I was out of school for a dental appointment.

Oddly enough, in the winter when all this was happening my dad's aspirations had become those of the typical Conservative target voter. He was thinking of buying a house.

The Greater London Council's housing policy had been conducted by Horace Cutler and the Conservatives since the GLC's inception in the sixties. They had pushed for huge house building projects in which some of the accommodation would be for sale to better-off council tenants; a way of encouraging people to move out of the ghettoes that many council estates had become. Under one of these schemes, houses and flats were built on the vast flat swathe of marshland east of Woolwich. It turned into a ghetto itself – a brutal-looking council estate built piecemeal since the 1960s. There were wide canals to drain it. Living next to water was supposed to calm people down.

Amsterdam it wasn't. In 1980 it remained uncompromisingly flat under a huge sky with few trees, too much concrete and almost no shops, cinemas, pubs or cafés. All the things that give an area a vibrant street life were absent. It was just thousands of hutches in which to go crazy. Not for nothing had Stanley Kubrick shot his film, A Clockwork Orange in Thamesmead.

Mum and dad were fed up with rentals and at the very end of the 1970s we were much better off. Dad was earning again and when my youngest sister started school my mum got a job at Cane Hill. Cane Hill was a term of abuse at school ('he's got a screw loose, wants to be in Cane Hill'). It was Croydon's Victorian asylum.

Thamesmead was next to the river, and we could afford it, so we prepared to make the move. Anywhere new would be good, I thought. We moved in May 1980. I would have to travel from Thamesmead to Welling, further out in Kent, for the first two years at secondary school, but instead I did exactly what I'd done in Croydon: bunked off a day or two every a week, and got buses into London.

Days after moving to Thamesmead, I sought out the local Catholic Church, St Paul's. It was a very modern church, in fact a little too modern for my mum as it was an ecumenical church where the Church of England, the Methodists and the Catholic Church shared the building. I introduced myself to the Catholic Priest, Father Clements and asked if I could serve on the altar. He readily agreed. He told me to come back the next day as the Queen would be visiting.

I was very excited. I had only read about Kings and Queens in books. Now I was going to see one in real life.

I hardly slept that night. I got to the church very early and Father Clements welcomed me with a broad smile and asked me lots of questions about my family history. I asked why there was a joint church, and repeated what my nanna and mother had told me about Protestants. He told me that the Catholic Church was the one true faith but added that Jesus would want us to be friendly towards other religions.

That seemed fair to me. Then word came that the Queen was ten minutes away. Everyone was flustered, but was calm by the time she arrived. Her Majesty walked past me with a smile as I bowed my head. I felt exhilerated. On my way home I thought about the Royal line of succession and how she was related to all those famous Kings and Queens I had read about. Little did I know I would meet her again three decades later at a reception for MPs and MEPs at Buckingham Palace.

The new school was boys' only. Football was my defence. One attraction was the game itself – playing it, getting good at it, but above all, following Liverpool. I had never been to that city and nor had anyone I knew, but a year or so earlier Liverpool had defeated a Belgian club in the European Cup Final and I'd watched it on TV. Kenny Dalglish scored the winning goal and instantly became my hero. On the day I'd been at my grandmother's in Harrow. Wembley wasn't far, and there was nothing else to do in that house so a passion developed.

Football gave me friends. Otherwise, I had already heard the word 'gay', though not applied to me. But it was only a matter of time. I used to let my hair grow as long as could and at twelve I looked delicate; adults sometimes mistook me for a girl. On one occasion I was sitting in the corner of a pub in Brixton with my mum and dad and I remember the barmaid saying 'is that your daughter?' Mum gave a nervous laugh and my dad was frowning. I felt embarrassed. It was almost as if someone had read my mind and knew my secret. Whenever anyone made this mistake in front of my dad he would haul me off to the barber immediately.

I dreaded those short-back and sides.

Gay, I knew, was odd. One day I walked down the hill into Camberwell after the orthodontic appointment and there on the newsstand by the corner was a stack of Gay Times. I must have blushed. I couldn't go near it. 'Gay' was not what I wanted. At the same time I was curious.

As often as I could, I'd get the bus into Woolwich and Greenwich and on out to Lewisham, where I could catch the 36 through Camberwell to Westminster. Sometimes I stopped off in Greenwich, a pretty old town next to the river where I could stare at the Cutty Sark and the Observatory and the National Maritime Museum. They cost nothing to enter and sometimes, when I thought I wouldn't get stopped, I went in. I also used to go to the library there. Thamesmead had a library and so did Woolwich, along with its lines of dignified, dark-brick barracks on the riverbank, and the squaddies on the streets. Towards the end of school hours, on the coldest days of winter, it wasn't obvious that I was bunking off. I'd read whole books, going back day after day. I borrowed books to take home, and I read about other cities, other countries, and English history.

London began at Woolwich, where there was a town centre and a market. Thamesmead didn't seem to me, like London at all. It was white, featureless, inert. The best thing about it was getting out – going with the family on the Woolwich Ferry to see my mum's sisters and our cousins who'd got rehoused out of London and lived in Essex, or getting the bus to Greenwich. I loved being next to the river. At school we had cross-country runs, out of Welling down to the Water Tower on the Thames and over Shooter's Hill. I liked that, because it meant not being stuck, somehow – going somewhere different relieved my perpetual anxiety about my gender. Generally, I was unhappy, I lacked confidence. Most people take their gender for granted and to have a conflict like this was like a constant questioning of who you really are.

At weekends I went wandering. Woolwich and Greenwich had foot tunnels left over from the days when working people had used them as a cheap river crossing to work on the docks or in the City. You could walk through the tunnels for nothing. It was an eerie experience if you were the only person down there. If you hollered, your voice wailed back like a banshee's howl, bouncing off the tiled walls. I just loved journeys.

I was always having arguments with my dad; typical teenage rebellions like not wanting to help him with the car, get a haircut, or tidy my room. Yet in some ways it seemed the worse I behaved the more I'd get away with. On one occasion I ran away and tried to sleep in an unfinished house. I went home half-frozen at around one in the morning, expecting a clip round the ear. Nothing was said. Perhaps my parents were trying to make sense of their odd child in the same way I was trying to make sense of my conflicted self.

In the West End, I'd see people a few years older than me who looked really strange. I liked that. Then one night on Top of the Pops there was 'Adam', in swashbuckling satin and lace with a startling stripe of white under kohl-ringed eyes, with the 'Ants'. I was ecstatic. Colour. History. 'Stand and deliver – your money or your life!' I had one close male friend at school and the two of us got hold of a pot of Nivea cream and made white stripes across our faces. I had an eyeliner pen and tried that – in fact I think he probably did too (not at all hygienic) – and we messed about with our hair.

I stared at myself in his bedroom mirror. I had achieved the required look, although you wouldn't wear it out in Thamesmead which was a National Front stronghold with plenty of skinheads. They swaggered about in gangs, south-east-Londoners with number two haircuts, heavy Doc Marten high-top boots, calf-length trousers held up by braces and an air of menace. If you wanted to get your head stamped on you'd yell 'Ball-'ead!' I didn't. I kept well away.

Now I had music, football, and my secret life of 'away days' from school; and I was experimenting with androgyny. I knew what was coming. My body would change. It would make me into a man and I wouldn't be able to stop it. Somehow, someway, I was going to find a way to be the real me. I desperately wanted information. I was not attracted to boys, but the only references I could find to any kind of gender mismatch like mine were in books and articles about homosexuality, so I read those.

It was impossible to express any of this to my parents. I couldn't have told them about my inner life as a girl when I was little, and even less, now, when teenage rebellion had begun. At a holiday camp when I was ten, dad and I got first prize in a 'Chip off the Old Block' contest because I looked exactly like a mini-him, with longer hair. At some level my dad must have known that football or not, his first-born son wasn't going to become said Chip in any form whatsoever. He persisted, though. He saw it as his job to turn me into an honest working bloke like him. The whole thing about haircuts was a battle, and now there was this thumping beat off the television and an obvious weirdo who called himself Adam Ant. Stupid, he thought.

'He's got makeup on. Tch –'

Dad's message couldn't have been clearer: messing about with the sex you were born was disgusting. Being different was showing off and dressing up like a nancy boy, well, that was repellent. 'Queers', to my Dad and everyone like him at the time, were Camp, as depicted on TV. Camp was Danny La Rue, a drag artist; Dick Emery, a vulgar comedian in the tradition of the pantomime Dame; John Inman, who minced and squealed as a shop assistant in 'Are you being Served?', and Larry Grayson, prancing hilariously and mugging to camera.

Were these suitable role models for any son of his? 'Expletive No.'

To me, entering my self-obsessed teenage years rather early, it just seemed that dad went out of his way to make scathing remarks about anything I liked. I found an old record player, a heavy Dansette in its case. I plugged it in and it worked. I hid it under my bed and started buying records. After a few weeks he walked into my room and saw it.

'Where'd you get that?'

'Off of a skip.'

'You never wanna use electrical stuff that's been chucked out- it could give you a shock.' He snapped down the switch on the wall. 'Look at that cord, lucky you haven't burned the place down.' He put both arms round the record player and picked it up.

'Dad leave it! I've got my music –'

'You are joking of course. It's a waste of electric.'

'No it isn't.'

'You don't pay the bills.' He was going through the door with it now.

'Where you putting it?'

'It's getting smashed. Then it goes out with the bins.'

He took a hammer to it. I heard him. I was miserable. Not alienated from my parents exactly; I was still close to them, especially my mum. But at moments like these I knew my way forward would have to be without them.

5 | I AM NOT ALONE

London is a good city in which to be an outsider. Travelling on my own made me streetwise and more grown up. I developed skills I wouldn't otherwise have. I didn't know the dangers of travelling alone but I didn't talk to strangers. Unless I really had an appointment at Camberwell on the day, I was skiving off, so I had something to hide. If it was warm enough I'd take my school blazer off, but I was never challenged for buying a child ticket. I was tallish, but there were taller boys in my class.

My parents never asked me about homework and I only did it if it interested me. They'd never done any of course. They never noticed. They wanted me to do well at school but they didn't have a clue how that was achieved. They always thought I must be doing well because I knew the answers to questions on 'Sale of the Century'. When my reports carried variations of 'does not apply himself' (which they always did) dad shouted and went up to the school but nothing ever happened.

On the surface, things were calm enough. But inside I was feeling really agitated about myself. I couldn't speak to anybody. Not the priest – 'Why did God put me in the wrong body, Father?' That'd get me reciting Hail Mary's for a month. Not my brother; he was too young. Not a female friend, because since we moved here I didn't have any.

In Croydon, at the mixed school where they knocked my teeth in, I had had girl friends and although I never had that conversation with any of them they must have picked up on something. One of them had asked me – in the context of her being a tomboy – are you a tomgirl?

'NO!' I said. 'Course not!'

33

Then, in 1981, I was deep in the 'News of the World' one Sunday when I read about somebody who had changed gender.

'Look,' I said to dad. He was dozing after his usual Sunday session at the pub. 'Did you see about her? This girl, she used to be a man.'

'What?'

'She used to be a man, look.' The picture of Caroline Cossey was very glamorous. 'JAMES BOND GIRL WAS A BOY' screamed the headline.

'Eugh. They're sick, those people, sick,' he said vehemently. He pointed at my mother, who was coming in from the kitchen with two mugs of tea at the time. 'THAT's a woman. That's natural. Women give birth. Those people are just sick in the head, living in a fantasy world.'

My mum looked faintly surprised and sat down. I looked down again at the article. 'She used to be on 3-2-1.'

'That's a pervert. It's perverted.'

But I felt incredibly happy. It made me realise that I was not alone. Until then I'd thought I was some kind of nutcase – that I was the only person in the world who felt like this. It was a wonderful feeling to know that I was not alone.

Mum blinked, slowly, like a lizard, and sipped her tea. Her body language suggested that any discussion or debate on the subject was futile and that she had chosen the path of least resistance, a kind of acceptance that said 'What can you do...'

I'd started going to football matches, Charlton and West Ham – or often say I was going to the match and instead be in London all day, people-watching and feeling free. I got deeper and deeper into deception. Mum and dad were complacent because I always came back safely.

After telling them I was going to a friends to do homework I'd go into London, take my blazer off, wear my shirt out, mess my hair, and try to look slightly alternative. Freedom, adulthood; it was like a drug: I wanted it more and more.

My dad's interest in football was zero. One time I'd gone to the last match of the season in May. It was a beautiful evening and I got home very late, probably close to midnight having spent hours wandering around the West End. Dad was waiting up.

'What time do you call this?'

'Sorry dad.'

'Where've you been?'

'At the match, but I missed the bus.'

'Right, that's it. No football matches for two months.'

I looked horrified, but as I flopped onto my bed and pulled the covers over my head I grinned. Of all the men in Thamesmead, only my dad wouldn't have remembered – in fact probably didn't even know – that football isn't played in the summer.

When I went to school I was disruptive, sometimes singing Adam Ant songs aloud in class. We used to get plus and minus marks for behaviour every week, and if you got anywhere near ten minus marks you got the cane. Of course I did. I was often caned and occasionally slippered. Then I broke the school record when I scored minus 22 and I didn't get caned. For several days I got awe and respect from the whole class.

'You're not evil,' said the teacher, although he looked a bit doubtful. 'You're a bright lad. You just need to sort yourself out.'

From time to time a teacher would try having a heart to heart with me. It never worked. Why would it? They were teachers. They knew their job but I baffled them. Teacher training had not prepared them for a pupil with suppressed difficulties about gender.

There was every incentive to stay on the bus. I turned up for exams and did well, which perversely annoyed the teachers because of my erratic presence in class. I didn't excel in every subject – Science and Woodwork were blind spots – but at Sociology, Geography, History, and English, I was alright. I read Sociology textbooks and I'd learned RE since I was four, so no problem there.

Money was getting tight at home. I mean, tighter than usual. There were holidays; a driving holiday in Ireland, which was really good, and Pontin's several times – Brean Sands in Somerset. For a while we'd had a caravan in the Isle of Sheppey. My parents' priority was paying the mortgage. At thirteen, and an unusually mature thirteen in certain ways, my priority was myself: looking unusual, yet looking for a way to fit in.

Dad was starting to call me lazy. I also got that from the teachers. Although I had my London excursions, my football and music, at home I was always in the corner of the sitting room, deep in a book, not wanting to talk to anybody. The TV was never off and six of us had to fit onto one three piece suite, so the last kid in had to sit on the floor. I was a stony presence, reading; getting on dad's nerves. 'Your room's like a bomb's hit it!' I shared a bedroom with my brother, but I was the one with all the stuff, spilling out of cupboards, kicked under the bed. I didn't want to go and clean it. On Saturdays, I vanished – 'Going up the park'. No way was I going to help my dad with the car. The thought of getting muck under my nails from an engine. Ugh.

That Christmas I got a battery-operated transistor radio. Maybe dad felt remorse about the record-player. On Christmas Day, I heard Tony Blackburn on Radio One playing Ru-dee, a message to you! Brilliant. I was bopping round the room.

The whole two-tone, Ska craze was reaching its height then and The Specials and Madness were only really good if you turned the volume up. At school, uniform was a thing of the past. It was all about labels. You had to wear an Argyle sweater or one labelled Pringle or Lacoste. If you wore flares, you got beaten up. I had huge issues with my parents about clothes. To them, trousers were trousers and you got them off the rack at Tesco's. I doggedly washed cars, bought the clothes I had to have – like straight 'waffle' trousers and a green bomber jacket with orange lining – and wore those.

Then in the summer of 1981 my nanna from Brixton died, in her seventies, of a brain tumour. My mum and dad had just taken over a fish and chip shop in Plumstead, on the way to Woolwich, and my brother and I were away at some Catholic kum-ba-yah campsite place in Essex. My brother took nanna's death very badly. I never cried but I was upset. She had done a good job of imparting her religion to me and I consoled myself by thinking 'She's in a better place'. She had been frail, ill and in pain. My mum was distraught, more than I'd ever seen her be.

So there was a sombre mood that autumn when we went home; everything had changed. Mum was miserable, dad was stressed and they were both working at the chip shop every evening and all day except Sundays and Mondays. Because I was now a third-year, I had to get a different bus to the Upper School. When I got home they were at the shop until nearly midnight, so I was left to my own devices, on trust. This was the point, when I was thirteen, where I started night-clubbing.

6 | MY SECRET LIFE

I attended King's College Hospital Dental Institute about once a month from 1979 to 1982. It took over two and a half years to align my teeth and jaw correctly. After every appointment I'd get on the bus and go and see my aunty in Brixton.

Everyone I saw in Camberwell Green from the bus would have turned heads in Thamesmead – African women in vivid blues and yellows with towering headdresses; white boys with Mohicans dyed shocking pink and Indian girls in exquisite gem-coloured saris. But here in inner London nobody looked twice; anybody could be different. It gave me an idea.

Why didn't I come in one day as a girl?

But how? When? The urge to have the release of being a woman had become so overwhelming that I was blinkered to the risks and dangers.

I kept my hair long, though schoolboys didn't then. My skin was pale; my hair was curly and flopped over my eyes. All I had to do was mess it up, wear my shirt askew and I'd look androgynous. We all had sports bags. I had a black nylon one with a discreet black Adidas logo. It could easily look like a big handbag.

I was five feet nine and passed easily for sixteen, except when I was in a school blazer. But how would I keep it secret?

Weeks went by. I saved some money. Luckily for me, the buses got cheaper when Ken Livingstone became leader of the GLC. You could go miles on a Red Rover ticket for 60p. I got a bus to Brixton one Saturday, slipped into the part of the market under the railway and bought a black dress. Brixton has always felt like a spiritual home for me – a place where those considered outsiders by the mainstream could easily fit in.

Back home, I tried it on, struggling with the zip. A tall, slim, angular girl, who was me, stared back from the mirror. I smiled in delight. Hurriedly I took the dress off and hid it under a pile of Smash Hits, stamp albums, football books and library books. Mum rarely disturbed that sort of thing. But there was always a worry it could be discovered, just as my record player was.

In the following weeks I purloined from my parents' room at different times a pair of American Tan tights, a pink lipstick and some pressed powder in a compact with a mirrored lid. My mum wouldn't miss one pair of tights and she hardly ever wore makeup unless she was going to a wedding or a christening.

The next KCH appointment was coming up. Mum and dad left for the fish and chip shop before I'd gone out. Everybody else went to school. In the empty house, I opened mum's wardrobe and took a pair of her size seven shoes with a low heel. She was three inches shorter than me, but I had small feet for my height and they fitted perfectly.

Wearing my school blazer, and carrying my girls clothes in the Adidas bag, I attended the orthodontic clinic. Afterwards I took the bus from Camberwell to Brixton as usual.

My aunty lived in a block of flats behind the Catholic Church. At the bottom of the block, there were some disused garages with rollover doors that were open. I walked into one. It was dark and smelly. There were filthy old sleeping bags and empty wine and beer bottles lying about. Entering as far as the light allowed, I shrugged out of my shirt and pulled the dress over my head. I then removed my trousers, rolled on the tights and zipped up the dress. I shoved my school clothes into my black bag. I moved closer to the garage entrance where the light was brighter – checking that nobody could see me – and I took out the 'borrowed' makeup compact, dabbed my nose with powder and applied a slash of the pink lipstick. For months, I'd been reading makeup advice in magazines – but this was the first time I had applied it.

My hair suitably mussed over my face, I stepped out.

For the first time in my life, I felt right; which was all I had ever wanted to feel. It wasn't a sexual thing: I had simply found the correct identity. I had a future here.

A thirty-second walk from the garage led me to a busy street. Nobody stared. I stood at the bus stop with a crowd of other people, mostly women, and got the first bus that came along. I paid full fare and the conductor made no comment. He barely looked at me.

I went in and out of shops along Oxford Street for more than an hour. Nobody stared. I bought a newspaper; the seller scarcely registered my existence. I was completely accepted as a girl.

I was happier than I had ever been; exultant. All my life I felt as if I'd been trapped in a darkened maze. Now, suddenly, I had found a way out into sunshine.

After a couple of hours I returned to the garage, wiped off the makeup, stashed the dress, put all my accessories into the bag and changed back into my school uniform and blazer. I then went upstairs to visit my aunt.

Looking back on those years I suppose my school friend, an equally fervent Adam Ant fan, was gay. We never had that conversation of course. I suppose it was fear. We knew that gay wasn't acceptable. He certainly had no idea that I ever wore girl's clothes, or that by the winter of '81 I'd done so several times. I had been scared in the Brixton garages so I found suitable women's public toilets and changed there. All I had to do was walk in looking androgynous and hope not to meet the same faces coming out. There was a particularly good Ladies at Catford.

My friend's parents cared about him but they seemed to understand that he needed some space. We were both, by then, reading iD magazine and The Face. They were full of impenetrable typography, quirky design, and images of ordinary people who looked bizarre but in a good way, as if they understood fashion. The pages were laid out in quirky bright colours and there were always photographs of cutting-edge kids off the street – boys with jet-black hair, wearing eyeliner and their granny's wartime fur coat, or girls with shocking pink lipstick, a feather boa, wedge-heeled high-tops and a polka-dot dress they'd run up themselves. In the gossip and opinion pages I found recurring names, usually adopted ones, like Princess Julia, or Steve Strange, who'd started Blitz club where Boy George had been a cloakroom attendant. I was no fan of Boy George, then or later, but I liked the look of everything that went on at the Blitz.

My dad gave me a reel to reel tape recorder with big speakers. My friend had a cassette player with two cassettes. You could mix tapes of your own. Buying music, mucking about with music, swapping it and listening to it; we did a lot of that. Most Saturdays I used to get a bus to Charlton or walk under the river from Woolwich and get a bus to West Ham to see a match.

Football and music kept me off the streets. The first time I got to see Liverpool play was the FA Charity Shield at Wembley in '82. I went all the way up there on a bus from London Bridge the week before to get my ticket. I'd got £6 together for it. I went on my own – my brother wasn't into football at that time.

Liverpool beat Tottenham one-nil, with a goal from Ian Rush in the 32nd minute. There was a lot of fighting that day. The Tottenham fans were notorious and running battles were almost expected. Every other time you went to a match you would see violence. There was a deafening chant –YOU'RE GOING HOME IN A RED AND WHITE AMBULANCE – racist chanting, homophobic chanting. Football was a very strange passion for me but it persisted.

Besides, I was going into the West End after matches at the weekend, and staying out after dark in the summer holidays, because I could. My parents were still shovelling cod and chips after the pubs shut. They were quite happy if I left before they did in the morning and stayed out all day. They weren't alone in this; most people then were pretty relaxed about their kids getting around on their own.

My friend and I liked the same kind of music, but he wouldn't join me when at thirteen I suggested we go clubbing. Yet again, I was on my own.

I had perfected one look that was unmistakably androgynous, and another that was entirely feminine. I chose androgyny that first time, with hair mussed and held together by loads of clips, and my face made up, with neat black lines of eyeliner trailing away from my eyes like the legs of immense spiders.

The Blitz Club was on Great Queen Street, off Kingsway, in the old terrace opposite the Freemasons' Hall. Covent Garden was not yet fully restored to glory after centuries of daytime life as a vegetable market and Kingsway was its furthest east edge. Over on the west edge, on the Charing Cross Road, was Central St Martin's School of Art where lots of Blitz people were students. Art students were cutting the cultural path ahead, as they'd been doing for decades.

I'd contrived to get from Thamesmead to Holborn tube at 10.30pm in term-time by claiming to be sleeping over at my friend's house.

I got to Great Queen Street to find that it was dark and rather austere with few pedestrians and the looming presence of Freemasons' Hall. Lights shone dimly from a few restaurants and a dark bar called Zanzibar.

There was no queue, just a notice on the door. Blitz had moved to the Camden Palace.

That was what you got in the days before Twitter; delayed communication – had I been in the loop already I'd have known – but I wouldn't find out until I got a copy of the Face.

I made it over to Camden, hair, spider eyes and all, though I actually felt a bit under-dressed once I got inside. Everybody was like me, and on the other hand, not like me. We were all outsiders in different ways, and fantastically dressed up, and it was easy to meet people and talk to them. In makeup, I was a boy or girl. People couldn't tell, although when they heard my light voice they probably thought I was a girl. About a third of the people there could have been either sex.

I went back. Not every week, because I couldn't manage that, but several times that winter. Occasionally I wore a dress, but other times I just pulled any old thing out of the cupboard and made it work. I wore jeans and a curtain once, off the shoulder and tightly belted.

People bought me drinks. But even at thirteen, I was careful. I was leading a triple or quadruple life, and I knew alcohol would do me no favours. When I was asked where lived I said Shooter's Hill or Greenwich (both of which were seriously upmarket of Thamesmead). I made out I was in sixth form at school. There were plenty of other kids there who were probably younger than they looked. People gave me their phone numbers and would ask for mine. I always told them I wasn't on the phone, which was not unusual then.

Once or twice I did phone somebody I had met there. Those conversations were uneasy on my part because I was laying claim to a life which at that time had no substance to it.

I had to lead a secret life. The people who really loved me didn't know me. I had to lie. I didn't feel good about it, or about thieving luncheon vouchers. My parents had the fish and chip shop open twelve- hours-a-day, five-days-a-week. They must have been exhausted. I look back on it now and I'm ashamed. At thirteen, most teenagers are focused on themselves and getting away. In that sense, at least, I was no different.

But if you lead a secret life, or several, there's a certain lack of commitment in all of them. As a schoolboy, I couldn't prevent my parents finding out when my absence from classes caused comment. I always promised not to do it again, but was warned I would be sent away if I did not pull my socks up. As a clubber, I couldn't see my new friends. There'd always be a party and I'd always have to lie – make up some reason why I couldn't go. I was getting approached. I looked 18, especially when I dressed as a girl.

I conducted what, at the time, seemed a logical thought process. I'm a woman, which means I must sleep with men. Therefore I decided to be attracted to them. I don't know if I naturally would have been, but I do know I made a conscious decision: 'that's what I do; that's what happens.' I was aware of gay people, but my role model was man/woman/family. I didn't identify as gay. I didn't dare confront the entire question of whether I was going to be a girl or a transvestite or what. All I knew was I wanted to attract men, so I started nicking cigarettes from my dad and smoking at Camden because I thought it made me look more sophisticated.

At home I was arguing with mum and dad. Teachers were getting more and more annoyed, but somewhere along the line, bizarrely, I'd internalised the model of the good Catholic girl. When men came on to me, I would never allow them to go any further than a kiss. I was drinking alcohol, but not much. I got tipsy. I kept my knees together and my buttons fastened.

On Sundays, with my frock safe in its hiding place and the makeup concealed in a pencil jar, I always arrived fresh faced and smiling at Church, where I would slip into a surplice and assist the priest at Mass.

By early '82 my school friend was also coming up to the West End with me during the day. Then came a day, early in February, that changed the course of my life.

He and I had got off the bus on Westminster Bridge because it was stuck in traffic, dodging across the road, deep in conversation, and walked round the corner into Whitehall. Up ahead, on the Downing Street side, people with banners had gathered and were shouting. There were journalists, cameras and police vans. I saw the words SAVE LAKER bobbing up on a handmade sign. The protest was about the fact Laker Airways had gone broke and those outside Downing Street

– shareholders or airline staff – wanted Margaret Thatcher and the Government to bail out the company.

Downing Street had scant security then – low iron gates that were more of a territorial marker, shut only at night. We sidled through the throng and got borne forward, past the police, towards the famous front door. I hadn't a clue what we were protesting about but it was a blast, being there, right in front of Number Ten, shouting SAVE LAKER for at least a minute until we were all shoved out again, still yelling, and the gates were shut.

We wandered around Soho until it was time to go back to Thamesmead. My parents would be at home because it was Monday, their day off. But that was not the end of it.

I was in my room at about ten to six that night when I heard my name bellowed from downstairs.

'GET DOWN HERE.'

My Dad stood at the bottom of the stairs, looking grim.

'What?'

'You 'eard. Get DOWN HERE.'

'Where were you today?'

'School.'

'No you bloody well weren't.'

'I was.'

'What were you doing in Downing Street?'

I probably blinked. 'School visit.'

'School visit, yeah? Yeah? Really? I just saw you on TV.' He'd been watching the 5.45 news. I'd been caught on camera. 'That's it. You've reached the end of the road this time.' My mum had come out of the kitchen.

46

'What's going on?'

'He's been skiving off. I've had enough. Shifty little bugger. He's going to be sent away to school, to knock some sense into him.'

'No he's not.' Mum had stopped dad sending me away before.

'Oh yes he is. He's no bloody good at school when he does go. He's going away.'

'I get good grades –'

'No you don't. You get Es. The best you ever get's a C.'

'That's only because they average the As with attendance and behaviour.'

'D'you think they don't matter? How you gonna keep a job if you don't bloody turn up? It's time you learned the facts of life.' He glowered at my mum. 'And don't you say another word. He's off.'

When my parents saw my end of term report my mother had said: 'we're going to show this to the priest.' They did, and he asked me about it. I reeled off the Ten Commandments and great chunks of the catechism. Afterwards he spoke to them, mildly. But this did not put an end to their frustration. That had been at Christmas.

So Dad's anger had been seething for a while, under the surface. He made an appointment to meet somebody at the Local Education Authority and told them I needed a short sharp lesson in a rigorous boarding school. There were further discussions, at which my existing school was represented. The word 'unmanageable' came into it.

I was told that I would leave at the end of the Spring Term and start the summer term at a Catholic boarding school for problem children.

'Where?' I asked.

'Just be certain it'll be a long way from here.'

7 | MORE THAN A MONTH IN THE COUNTRY

Blackthorn sprouted from the hedges and fresh green leaves sparkled in sunlight above. Deep country lanes wound through remote villages. The mini-bus turned into a lane, rocked down a track, and pulled up outside a gothic Victorian mansion with lots of outbuildings in Gloucestershire.

Despite my initial trepidation the staff were welcoming.

I was shown into a dormitory with eight beds. There was a tall cupboard in which I would keep my things.

For the first few days I pretended this wasn't happening. I hardly spoke. I missed London. My parents would not be allowed to visit for four weeks. I missed them too, although not enough to let them know who I really was. Before I left I'd collected everything that might betray me: eyeliner, bracelets, two or three dresses that had been neatly folded in boxes under deep piles of LPs. I took it all out and dumped the whole lot in waste bins.

The emotional baggage I brought with me to boarding school included fury, worry, self-consciousness, vanity and resentment. Fear, too. I had been dreading something like a Christian brothers outfit with beatings.

But these were not Christian brothers – in fact some were women. They looked no different from any other adults and some were in their twenties. They were here to promote my intellectual and social development as a productive member of society. As long as I stuck to their fairly rigorous routine they would find something to keep me interested. I'd had some good teachers before – but school had been wrecked in spite of them because I was always picked on or isolated.

49

Children somehow knew that I was different in a way that disturbed them. Here, the teachers were vigilant and bullying was never tolerated.

I began to reconcile myself to my situation.

We had breakfast at 8.30 and housework at 9, with our own designated job. School started at 9.30 but we didn't finish till 4.15. So our school day was longer than most, but nearly all our free time was occupied and there were no more than eight students to a class. There was a library, a swimming pool, badminton, football, guided walks, school visits, and never more than about 55 pupils in the whole school. We were organised in House units with thirteen or fourteen children in each, and a House Father and House Mother with a couple of other adults, so every House was a kind of family. You were expected to write to your parents (or in some cases, guardians) every week. You got weekly pocket money, a set amount according to your age.

Within days I had begun to mellow. In about a week, I absolutely loved it. At last I had found a school that nurtured me. Where I fitted in. I wasn't identified as a delinquent, but as a motivated student.

The routine was comforting. There was a set time for everything. The discipline was not the 'Do as I say' sort that I was used to. It was the kind that enables you to go forward and encourages you to make every minute count.

Until now, with the exception of religious instruction, I'd been largely self-educated by my own random, undirected reading. But Maths is not something you can teach yourself. Mrs MacDonald sat down and taught me fractions in ten minutes and told me I was the quickest student she'd ever taught. I felt empowered, more confident. If there was something I didn't understand, I could trust her to explain it to me. I stopped dreading Maths. In fact I didn't dread any of the lessons. I had to catch up with a lot of them, and on the whole, I succeeded; next term I could start studying for O levels.

I went home for half-term. My parents seemed really guilty about sending me away, my mother especially, but she was distracted that particular week – at the end of May – by the imminent arrival of Pope John Paul II. Not at our front door in Thamesmead exactly, but not far away. We were going to see him.

The Pope turned up at Gatwick, where he was met by a Cardinal and an Anglican bishop, and got the train to Victoria. We were in the crowd that filled the square outside Westminster Cathedral. My, how things had changed. In the course of this visit the Pope met the Queen and visited Canterbury Cathedral where he prayed with the Archbishop. Mum didn't turn a hair. She'd assimilated (I knew about assimilation from Sociology classes) but at the same time, when she wanted to know something dad couldn't tell her, she'd still go straight to the priest. We saw His Holiness again at Wembley Stadium. There was a homily and prayers. Just being there was exciting. History was being made.

Back at school, I was untroubled because I was busy. The teachers noticed if you couldn't keep up and spent time with you – after school if necessary. I watched TV, especially the news, as I had at home. The Falklands War had begun and lead every bulletin. The staff left their newspapers in the living room at the House. I read the Daily Mail, Daily Express, The Times and the Guardian. There was no News of the World or the Sun.

This was the height of Margaret Thatcher's popularity. I drank in her constantly repeated refrain – Stand on your Own Two Feet. She applied it to Britain, standing up to the bullying generals in Argentina; I applied it to myself. You couldn't expect other people to do things for you. It was nice if they did, as adults were doing things for me now, but if ever I felt tempted to become dependent on the approval of others, I must resist.

I thought that was right. Margaret Thatcher was a strong role model and I knew I had to take her advice if I was ever going to be the person I wanted to be.

I stopped thinking about how my change from male to female could be achieved. Boarding school filled my day with events and a structure. I began training for the Duke of Edinburgh awards. In my two years at that school, I learned abseiling, pot-holing and water ski-ing. We went to Ross on Wye and camped at Symonds Yat, bird-watched at Slimbridge, hiked in the Brecon Beacons, learned orienteering in the Forest of Dean and took regular long country walks. We got an immense amount of life experience, learned to listen to instructions, learned to wonder and look for answers. Most of us were city kids who got there barely knowing an oak from a toadstool. We'd never seen peregrine falcons or hedgehogs before, far less climbed mountain tracks or waded through streams. We had never had to test our own capacity to survive in the natural world.

One of the Housemasters had been a Royal Marine. I excelled at swimming. I got my Lifesaver bronze and silver medal and started training for my gold.

My July school report, at the end of the first term, showed straight A's. My dad was so pleased that he gave me a fiver – a big, crisp blue fiver – in spite of my long, curly hair that I didn't want to have cut. We compromised; I promised him that I would get it cut before I went back. For two years afterwards, I started every term with short back and sides and ended it with wild curls. In the holidays, I would buy dresses in Brixton Market, wear them out a few times clubbing or during the day, and at the end of term, I'd have to dump them.

When the autumn term started, my mum secretly sent me money at school. I think she was uneasy about me being so far away. Not that it didn't make our family the object of envy. A kid at boarding school? 'Stuck up cow.' Social aspirations didn't go down well where we lived.

The school offered far more than an education: it offered security. The teachers had a pastoral, parental role, and knew how to supervise from a distance. We were trusted. Also, because I was fourteen now, we were allowed out on Saturdays and we could smoke. When mum's first letter arrived with money in it, I bought a packet of ten cigarettes from the shop in the village. I sloped off to the smoking area after tea, lit one of them, and inwardly admitted that the sensation was disappointing.

With my Irish Nanna
Visiting my Cousin in hospital

In my paternal
Grandmother's arms

Me and My Dad

Winning the "Chip off the old
block" competition

Pontins, May 1979

In Lourdes with My Mum

Summer 1991

Clubbing in Cyprus, 1993

Outside Templeman library
University of Kent 1998

In Cyprus, months before surgery

Just a few friends
during the Oz
tour

Canberra, July
1998

On the
Las Vegas strip
August 1998

Sydney's Olympic pool
June 1998

Ecstatic after swimming with dolphins on
my 30th birthday

Campaigning early in my UKIP career

Always loving a party

Celebrating the success of the '99 European election at UKIP Head Office

Fabian - the "Humble toiler in the Vineyard". My UKIP soulmate

I looked at the burning tip, the smoke rising. What a waste of money.

I decided to give up. I had nine left. I could sell them in ones. I could sell them now.

This developed into a profitable little trade. I wasn't making a fortune, just two or three pounds a week. I had a Barclays Supersaver account with a miniature Barclays safe, and at fourteen you could go into Gloucester on Saturdays if you wanted. I could bank there or take money out. I would buy a pair of trousers, or Kenny Dalglish silver football boots. I bought nearly all my own clothes; my parents' idea of what was suitable having remained wildly at variance with anything I or anyone else my age would actually wear. My pride and joy was my red Liverpool replica shirt, just like Kenny's. I would try and wear it all the time, even waiting for it to dry on the radiator.

I bought myself a Walkman, but after half-term I let my pocket money build up for Christmas in my Supersaver account. Underneath the posing and the bolshiness I definitely had a canny, petit-bourgeois streak. Mrs T would have loved me. Even if I did (at times other than Christmas) head for Barclays in Woolwich at the start of every holiday and withdraw cash to spend on glamour from Brixton Market.

Soon it was Easter again. In June 1983 there was to be a General Election. The outcome was not in doubt. In the back of the fish shop, where I was working in the holidays, Radio One played a clip from the previous year's Labour conference where a woman had taken the podium. 'I stand here proudly as a lesbian', she said. A nail in Labour's electoral coffin. Then there was Greenham Common where, as the media never ceased to remind us, the women all wore dungarees, didn't wash, and were strident. What with all this, plus internal squabbles and takeovers by Militant and a mad-looking old intellectual in charge, Labour was identified with just about everything that made the white working class uncomfortable.

As a firm Thatcherite, I was going to do my bit to support her in any case. At half term I walked into the Woolwich Conservative party's HQ and asked if I could deliver leaflets. I wasn't yet fifteen, but I was tall and confident and hey, I went to boarding school, and they welcomed my assistance.

It was probably the second most low-key General Election I've ever been involved in. I went out knocking on doors for a week, but most of the time I was preaching to the converted. Election results normally come in late at night, and with re-counts and hotly contested marginals you can expect to be awake until four. I had my little transistor radio with an earphone and lay in bed listening. I only had to wait until about one o'clock before I knew the Conservatives had won decisively.

Since I was ten I had wistfully wanted to be a politician but suspected that I never could. Now I was certain that my private life would be unacceptable. I had never forgotten dad's disgust about Caroline Cossey, still the only person I had ever read about who had somehow – I didn't know how – changed sex. Prior to this General Election, I had seen what happened to Peter Tatchell. He was not a woman in a man's body, but a homosexual, of whom there were millions, and the Labour candidate in one of the safest Labour seats in the country – white working-class, council-estate, former-docker, market-porter, Bermondsey. Despite having campaigned for years for gay rights, he refused to talk to journalists about his own sexuality. Unpleasant things were put through his letter-box. He even got death threats. The Liberals ran a dirty campaign of insinuation and sneering and beat Tatchell by a mile.

I didn't think of myself as gay. I was a lot more complicated. I could never go through what he had. But what would become of me? I was still religious, but knew I wasn't the priest type. I was pretty sure I wouldn't make a sailor, either, another idea I had toyed with. Yet all the physical changes had begun. I wasn't getting a hairy chest or even a hairy face, but I was still in the body of a boy, and the tallest in my class; six feet tall by my fifteenth birthday.

I distracted myself. I still read History for amusement. Mrs MacDonald announced in class that we were going to visit Berkeley Castle, where Edward II died, followed by Gloucester Cathedral, where he was buried. I remembered reading about that King and his boyfriends.

'Does anybody know how Edward II came to die there?' she asked.

We didn't. So she walked around the room telling us all about the Plantagenet King Edward II; how he'd been a hopelessly disorganised and spoiled king who made favourites of some of his courtiers. One in particular, Piers Gaveston, seemed to be able to manipulate the King and they were said to be having a homosexual relationship. Queen Isabella got fed up with Edward II because he was always out having a good time with Piers Gaveston and paid her no attention. He hadn't been all bad – he'd had a bash at defeating the Scots at Bannockburn – but in the end Isabella and her lover invaded England and overthrew him. He was imprisoned in Berkeley Castle all through the summer of 1327, and suddenly he died there.

'Nobody knew what killed him,' Mrs MacDonald concluded, as she walked past me, 'but it was said to be a red-hot poker up the posterior.'

'What's that?' I said.

She lowered her voice to a dramatic whisper. 'Up the bum,' she said.

I was horrified. It was like a lesson in the violence some people used, and still did, towards those of whom they didn't approve; those who were different. We went to Berkeley Castle and peered down, down, into the horrible dungeon he'd died in. I felt sick.

The sheer drama of all the undiscovered knowledge kept me going. In class we read To Kill a Mockingbird, Lord of the Flies, Cider with Rosie, *which was set in what was now well-loved Gloucestershire territory, and* The Grapes of Wrath. *There was an underlying political message in most of what we read and when we discussed them our teachers rewarded us with respect and interest, instead of the usual dull 'read this, listen to what you'll get examined on, and make a note' that I'd been used to.*

Half a dozen of us were loaded into a minibus to go and see JB Priestley's 'Dangerous Corners' in Cheltenham. For most of us, me included, it was our first visit to the theatre. We went to see a performance of Cats in the West End and saw 'Blood Brothers' in Bath. Bigger groups were bussed to Stratford-upon-Avon to see the RSC's 'Twelfth Night' and 'A Midsummer Night's Dream'. I was enchanted; I didn't understand every word but I loved it. Shakespeare's plots were full of people dressing up and acting the wrong sex.

Shortly after we saw 'The Merchant of Venice', an old gentleman came to talk to us. He was a Treblinka survivor, modest, gentle, matter-of-fact, yet he recalled cruelties beyond belief. I was in tears. Nobody could have made the Holocaust as horrifying, as immediate, as that man, to kids born more than two decades after the event.

We read AJP Taylor and Winston Churchill on the Second World War. Mr Lynch, my History teacher, had been a navigator on Lancaster bombers. I was privileged to meet people of that generation. If I hadn't gone to that school our paths would never have crossed. Our teachers didn't knock off and go home, they stayed. They engaged with us. Mrs Meadows and Mrs MacDonald in particular gave so much time to us. For the first time I could discuss what I was learning and feel I was listened to.

I was going in for County swimming trials and I was exceptionally good at badminton: I'd never seen, far less picked up, a badminton racquet before I went to that school. A generous teacher paid for me to go with a group to Bulgaria and learn ski-ing. I didn't like the ski-ing much, and wasn't very good at it, but I was interested in a way of life where 'normal' didn't mean what it did back home. We got off the plane in Sofia, and there was a big old tank on the tarmac. Crowds of middle-aged men came forward wanting to buy our clothes off our backs.

There seemed no limit to the things we could do. In my second year there, Bryn Phillips, the Welsh ex-international Rugby player who took us for Geography and PE, sat down and taught me about maps:

how to understand contour lines and shipping routes, find places, and how longitude and latitude related to distance and the speed of the earth's rotation around the Sun. I hadn't grasped all this before.

After that I spent hours and hours with maps, mostly of Europe and the USA, planning journeys I intended to take. Most of Eastern Europe, and all of China, was off limits then, behind the Iron Curtain. But taking a gap year for travel was becoming common. A generation before, nearly every kid who stayed at school until they were eighteen either got a job right away or went on without a break to a training college or university. Now all the long-haul airlines sold round-the-world tickets valid for a year, discounted for students. The trail was thick with backpackers: Kathmandu or Goa, Bangkok or Bali, Australia, New Zealand, Hawaii, the West Coast, New York. Every sixth-former knew about Greyhound buses and Eurorail passes. One of the junior staff members had a girlfriend in LA and he told us how he'd met her when he was backpacking in America.

Somehow, my aspirations – which had been variable and nebulous in London – were starting to fall into place. After A levels, I'd get a good job, or maybe even go to a university or a polytechnic: you could get grants, then, for tutorial fees and accommodation. And I didn't know what I would work as, but it would give me an income sufficient to travel the world.

In these two years I learned that if you wanted something enough, and you worked hard enough, you could do anything you wanted. At my last school, when I told a teacher that I wanted to be a politician she'd led the whole class in an outburst of laughter. Here there were never any messages about limitations. Respect, enabling, choice – the key was positivity. With something to aim for, I kept my grades up all the time.

Partly because of glowing reports and partly because mum felt so guilty, I could do pretty much as I liked in the holidays. If dad got annoyed or suspicious, my all-conquering, Dah-Dah! get-out-of-jail-free card appeared every Sunday to make him think better of it: I was a devoted altar server, always on time for Mass.

So when I was home, I stayed out at nights by claiming to be at a friend's house. I wanted to keep the boundaries stretched. I had more money and had graduated from buses to trains. There was no railway station at Thamesmead. (What had the GLC been thinking, housing scores of thousands of people without extending the line?) To get into London, you had to get to Woolwich by bus. You could cross the river by the foot tunnel or on the Woolwich Free Ferry and catch a train to Liverpool Street and the City, or you could get a train straight out of Woolwich to Charing Cross. The rolling stock was old, with individual compartments. If you couldn't find an empty one, there were carriages with corridors and a loo at the end. I became expert in knowing exactly where on the platform the single-compartment carriages would stop, and I knew the timing between stations; if I had to, I could do a complete dress, hairdo and makeup in the six minutes between Deptford and London Bridge.

I'd go to a club and get the paper train back at three or four in the morning – in those days, most clubs shut at about two. When, occasionally, strangers hit on me, late at night on the train, nothing serious ever happened. My biggest problem was washing off my makeup.

I had friends of both sexes when I went out, but people who went to Camden every week were seeing each other at other clubs as well. I wasn't part of that scene because I wasn't a regular, but I'd get invited back to parties. Since I nearly always went out on Tuesday nights, my parents would have gone to work when I got home. Once I woke up at seven in the morning in a roomful of people dozing. I staggered into the kitchen and found somebody making coffee.

'Where am I?'

'Maida Vale.'

'Where's that?'

I'd never heard of it. I walked out, saw a main road and a big red bus, and got to Trafalgar Square in about fifteen minutes. Commuters were bursting out of packed trains coming into Charing Cross.

When I got home the house was empty. My siblings were at school and my parents at the chip shop.

Then, in the autumn term of '83, two unrelated things happened. I became a prefect, and I started to have sex.

As a prefect I could confiscate cigarettes from Juniors if I caught them smoking, which I frequently did. All of a sudden my part-time business had no overheads. Did the staff never find out? I think they knew, but everyone benefited. It was never a big deal because I wasn't the only one doing it.

As to the sex, I was underwhelmed. The boy and I were both fourteen and I didn't even particularly like him. It had started when we had a ridiculous conversation on the bus home for the start of the Easter holidays.

'Are you gay?'

'No.'

'If you say you're gay I'll say I'm gay.'

It was a bit scary because somehow we both accepted the fact that we were not heterosexual males, but I didn't know if gay quite related to me. In the end I accepted that category, not knowing a different one.

The good thing was, he didn't tell anyone and nor did I. So we had a secret. That autumn term, one night in the dormitory he crept into my bed. Nobody knew. As far as the rest of the school was concerned, we weren't even friends. It wasn't regular although it went on happening occasionally.

I'd begun to understand how difficult life was going to be. I was a quiet, diligent pupil, and still a prefect. I loved being at school.

However, anxiety had returned. By Christmas I was six feet two. This made it rather more difficult to look like a girl. In the spring term of '84, I bought myself some new trousers and three weeks later they were too short.

The staff knew I was devout and let me and a few others attend a vigil mass in a Roman Catholic church in Gloucester. This meant staying up all night between Saturday and Sunday. Another boy and I snuck out on the Saturday evening. We went into a pub together but he looked younger than I did, so I was the one who ordered a pint of lager and lime. The bar staff didn't turn a hair, and I carried it outside to where people were drinking at tables.

We were sharing the drink when I heard: 'Good evening, boys.' I looked up and saw the priest from the church. We were reported to the school. This misdemeanour (so uncharacteristic they thought) shocked the teachers. I think they thought I had been led astray.

Not long before the end of the spring term, a letter arrived from the Local Education Authority. They would pay for my further education. In the autumn I'd continue to board here, but do my A levels at a college in Gloucester. The Headmaster and the teachers were delighted. They had taken a disruptive truant and under-achiever, and in two years had changed his whole outlook on life.

I was ecstatic, mainly with relief. School, which from the age of five I had loathed and despised, had now become my security blanket. It was a safe base from which my problems might be resolved.

The LEA's letter was congratulatory. I was expected to pass half a dozen O levels and continue, probably to degree level. None of my cousins had achieved anything but I knew I would. And I would be a student, for which I was deeply grateful. There was nothing I wanted less than to be a lorry driver or work on a building site. That wouldn't happen now. My dad had always said it was one of the biggest regrets of his life that he'd left school too early. He'd been a boarder like me but one day, just before his fifteenth birthday, the age at which in his day you could leave school, his father and stepmother visited and told him he had to get a job.

And yet – here I was, about to be sixteen, and the LEA were willing to pay quite a lot of money to educate me for two more years. At Easter I revised for my O levels in Woolwich Library.

It was at a desk there one day that I noticed a thin red book, lying on top of a row of others on a shelf. I peered at the spine. Homosexuality, Transvestism and Change of Sex.

The author Eugene de Savitsch, MD, told me everything I had always wanted to know but had been afraid to ask, in a matter-of-fact and sympathetic style. His book had been published in the United States in 1958, a time when homosexual 'practices' were illegal and public vilification total. Dr Savitsch's liberal attitude was way before its time. He cited the British Wolfenden Report. Nothing similar had been commissioned in the US. Certainly he called homosexuality an 'abnormality', but his view was clear: it was in no way criminal, and it was not a choice but a natural predisposition. He made a clear moral distinction between regular homosexuals and pederasts who preyed on boys.

None of this concerned me quite as much as the 'change of sex' part. I skipped through the bit on hermaphrodites before I came to;

'There is also a fairly large group where...the 'psyche' may be quite different from the predominant sexual characteristics. Indeed, in these cases the body may be essentially that of the male but the sexual impulse predominantly that of the female, and vice versa.'

Hmm. Still not quite me. There was a lot more than sexual impulse going on in my psyche. He wrote about chromosomes. My eyes began to glaze over. I read about androgyny in males, where some of the secondary sexual characteristics like slightly large breasts and hips, or lack of body hair, might be present but everything depended on hormones. 'The knowledge of hormones is becoming daily more and more precise and in fact a new speciality, 'endocrinology', the study of the glands of internal secretions, constitutes an important part of the medical curriculum', he wrote.

But surely I hadn't had dodgy hormones when I started dreaming of being a girl? I had been five. Nothing entirely matched.

The important thing confirmed by Dr Savitsch was that there was an operation. The off-putting thing was that the more you read about the people who'd had it, in the first part of the twentieth century, the more you realised that there was real disturbance here. One man had tried to remove his own penis with 'a piece of knotted string'. I gasped; I winced. I looked up from the page. Nobody in the library had noticed my horror. When these individuals got what they wanted – namely, breasts and a vagina – they were in general delighted, albeit living in reduced circumstances because of being female and losing their jobs. Most of them had been depressed for decades before, not because they had a congenital mental illness but because their inner conflict caused them such torment.

I didn't want to delay this. I wanted to find out how it could be done for me before I ended up a disturbed, tragic adult. But I had heterosexual friends and read the papers. I knew that doctors were forever breaking their trust and informing the parents of girls who'd asked, in confidence, for the contraceptive pill. Some doctors, especially Catholic ones, felt compelled to do this if the child hadn't reached the age of consent, which (for heterosexuals) was sixteen.

I would be sixteen in less than four months. I could wait.

In the first half of the summer term we sat our O levels, and afterwards for me there was real excitement: a trip to Lourdes. I had been picked to represent the school as a helper when the Children's Pilgrimage Trust took some handicapped and underprivileged children there.

The flight from Gatwick was my first time in a plane. I sat beside an eighteen-year-old helper called Angela. I loved the whole experience of Lourdes, the mountains, the basilica, the grotto and the endless trail of pilgrims in the sunshine. Every day we attended Mass with the children in their wheelchairs. They were sweet. Angela, though, developed a big crush on me. She clung. She was nice, but I'd never been a girl's boyfriend before and I did not feel at all comfortable. We kissed, and kept in touch for a while, but nothing else happened.

I arrived home during half-term. Mum was out at the shops. Dad had finished filling in a form at the table, pushed it into its envelope and put the biro down.

'Six more weeks of school,' he said to me.

'Yeah.'

'What are you going to do then?'

'I dunno.'

'Well you wanna start thinking about it.'

'What, the holidays?' Strange question he'd asked. There were summer holidays every year, but I never did anything in them that I'd choose to discuss with my parents.

'Not for the holidays! It's time you got a job.'

'But I'm only off till September.'

'Where d'you get that idea?'

'You saw the letter, I'm doing A levels.'

'Oh yeah? I can see the attraction of dossing for another two years but it ain't gonna happen.'

'What? But I'm going to do A levels! It's work.'

'Work! If you think that's work you need a short sharp shock. You need to be earning.'

'What's mum say?'

'Never mind that. You want toughening up. It's a hard world. Soon as you're sixteen, you're off down the Labour Exchange.'

'I could go to University!'

'Phh, and the rest. You think I'm going to slave my guts out while you go through the next four or five years without bringing any money in, you're off your rocker. University! Who do you think pays for that?'

'They'll pay for me.'

'In term time, yeah. You'd be here four months a year, eating us out of house and home. You know you're going to have to pay rent to your mother. You won't be able to claim.'

'Rent? To pay rent here? I don't believe this.'

'You'll be sixteen. That's adult. You don't get board and lodging for nothing when you're sixteen. I'd been working a year at your age. I know you. You just wanna stay up there because you're scared.'

That was sort of true. I didn't understand my own identity so I didn't have a plan.

'You're sixteen at the end of next month. You're going down the town and signing on.'

8 | YOU'LL GROW OUT OF IT

I got 80p an hour, standing at a machine doing the same three hand movements for eight hours at a time, with thirty minutes for lunch and an occasional tea break. Something saleable emerged at the end of the production line – though what it was I neither knew nor cared. The factory smelled of machine oil and plastic. A day there felt like a month.

I had signed up for a Youth Training Scheme but I couldn't start until September. The rent needed paying so I'd got this factory job. It was August and sunny outside; the O level results weren't in yet.

I was depressed, initially by shock. I had loved that school. The Headmaster and the teachers were dismayed when I told them I wasn't going back. I'd thought I had a future, and so had they. Only my parents didn't believe in me. At the time, I didn't understand that there was nothing personally insulting about that. They lived under a low ceiling and expected their children to do the same. My mum had wanted me to stay on – she'd fought hard for me, and lost to my dad – but even she didn't see the point of me getting an education. She wanted me in Gloucestershire because up there I'd be out of trouble. My brother was giving them grief. Thamesmead had problems with drugs and drink and abuse. At school I was secure.

Never give up, I thought. Sometimes it felt hard to stick to this mantra. I signed up for two evening classes in A Level English and History at Woolwich. My mum paid – it was £10 for each course. I would take the exams in two years' time but the courses, one night a week each, didn't start for a month.

In the meantime, here I was with zero mental stimulation and no social life. I was doing a 40-hour week for £32, my rent was £15, my bus pass was £3, and the bus ride morning and evening took forty-five minutes with a walk at both ends. All the fun I'd had before was gone. I was exhausted and deadened by disappointment.

I was now sixteen, the age I was told I could see a doctor about my gender problems with no fear that it would get back to my parents.

I hadn't seen our doctor since my only visit when we first moved to Thamesmead. She was about forty, pleasant-looking, and not at all intimidating as she sat behind her desk with a notepad. Beside her telephone, in a silver frame, was a studio photograph of two beaming little blonde boys of nine or ten in snowy shirts.

'Good morning, you're bright and early. So what can I do for you?' she asked.

'Umm... It's something that's been bothering me for a long time. 'I mean since I was about three. I don't want my parents to know.'

'I won't tell your parents.'

I trusted her. 'I've always felt I'm in the wrong body.' She blinked. I rushed on. 'I've been having this dream since I was about five. I wake up and everything is all right because I'm a girl. I know I should be a girl. I'm really depressed because I'm only happy when I'm wearing girl's clothes. I've been going to clubs since I was thirteen, as a girl.'

She looked baffled. 'What sort of clubs?'

'Night clubs, you know, in the West End. Inside I am a girl. I've never wanted to fight anybody or do any of the jobs my dad does. I look to other women for my role models. I am in the wrong body and I've read this book. I know you can get it done. You can get surgery. There's a woman called Caroline Cossey – she did it – I just don't know how to start. But I know being a man is making me depressed. I want to be referred for surgery.'

She paused. 'Hold on a minute. How old are you?'

'Sixteen.'

'I thought so. Look, calm down, don't be silly. You're still going through puberty.' To add to my woes, my face had erupted in spots. 'We all have an identity crisis during puberty. It's a hormonal thing. You'll grow out of it.'

'I can't grow out of it if it's me. I've been dressing as a girl. I've been seeing men – I'm only happy as a girl. Looking like this I feel all wrong.'

'Don't be silly. You're a great strapping lad. How tall are you?'

She measured me against a chart in the corner.

'Six foot four. Not petite, exactly, are you? You're physically normal. I've looked at your notes. I last saw you when you were twelve. You were a boy then, and there's nothing in your notes to say otherwise. You've developed normally, physically?'

'Yes.'

She sighed. 'You know this is a fantasy, don't you? Come and sit down again.'

I sat facing her. 'It isn't a fantasy. I've read about people who've done it.'

'Where do you get these ideas?'

'Caroline Cossey was a Bond girl, she looks amazing. She used to be a man.'

'Look. You have to get a grip. This is someone in a magazine. Everyday life is not glamorous. You can't just get what you want. Fantasies are exactly that. You can't just walk into your GP's surgery and she'll write you a note about a sex change. You didn't honestly expect me to do that did you?'

I didn't dare say that I had. I felt stupid. 'No.'

'And if you carry on like this, picking up men when you're dressed as a woman, there is every likelihood that you'll end up living on the streets of London as a drug addict or a prostitute.'

Clonk.

'But —'

'Do you not see the sense of what I have just said?' I was silent.
'You are indulging in an adolescent fantasy. You are grown up now,
you're a young man. You were born male. Do you see that for the sake
of your own future happiness you must face up to that?'

'Yes, I suppose so.'

'I'm sorry to disappoint you but it makes sense, doesn't it?'

'Yes.' I felt as if all the muscles in my face were collapsing, as if I
had suddenly turned fifty. All the things I'd ever dreamed about — living
in France or America, or going to China — had been ripped away from
me. Life was going to be exactly like this: impoverished, grey, wrong.
I was trapped. 'Yes. Yeah, I see what you mean.'

I left the surgery and walked to a bus stop. I got on a bus. I sat on
the top deck, quietly crying, and stayed on it until it got to the terminus.
Then I returned to the factory, late for work.

My hair was greasy, my face was spotty, and sexual things were
happening to me that I neither understood nor wanted; I felt
repugnance about my own body.

I was not suicidal — though people do get like that. In other
countries, people are punished — castrated or murdered, even as small
children — for revealing what I had just told the doctor. She would not
tell anyone, but at the same time she had plunged me into despair. For
if I believed what she told me, then all hope had gone.

Never give up. Somehow I had to keep believing that one day I
would be able to get what I so wanted and needed.

Being at home was getting me down. I looked for somewhere else
to live, but gave up. Renting a flat cost a fortune and I had never heard
of housing benefit. I didn't know that when you were sixteen and
'vulnerable' (being gay made you vulnerable to being thrown out of

home) you could get this benefit from so-called 'Loony Left' councils like ours in Greenwich.

I had given up, caved in to dad, and got this dead-end job because I thought I had to, because I wanted to prove I wasn't lazy and because I thought at least having some money of my own would be a relief.

I'd made the decision, albeit under pressure. And here I was, stuck.

My O level results came through, and were good; A's in History and Religious Education, B's in English and Sociology, and C's in Maths, Geography, and Human Biology. The YTS course started, and the A level courses. The Youth Training Scheme paid £26.25 a week, plus a subsidised transport pass. I studied for an ITEC with 20 other sixteen and seventeen-year-olds. We were to emerge computer-literate.

The YTS course was in Woolwich and so were the evening classes. I had homework but I also found a part-time job in McDonalds in Bexleyheath. At work my curls were tucked under a cap. At home, my dad was irritated at the sight of me because this year he hadn't been able to force me to the barber's. 'Going out like that? Look like a pansy.' I became indifferent to his comments. I was paying rent now and could do what I liked.

I was still going to libraries. The ones run by Greenwich Council took Gay Times and I used to read it. Often you would pick it off the shelf and it had been ripped in half. Once there was a razor in it and another time there was writing – WEVE SEEN YOU PICKING THIS UP YOU QUEER WHEN YOU LEVE HERE YOUR DEAD. (sic). That's how it was in 1984. The bigots couldn't punctuate or spell.

It was in Gay Times that I saw advertisements for different groups; there were clubs for gay men, youths and lesbians. I decided to attend one for youths, in Catford. I was desperate to find a compromise between the way I felt and what the doctor had said, because her opinion would lead straight to marriage to a woman, 2.4 children and a council house – and I definitely wasn't having that.

I'd begun to think that if I could just be a gay man, maybe I would be alright. I went to the group a few times and later that winter became involved with an older man who lived on the Isle of Dogs. He was friendly and about thirty years older than me. Maybe I was lonely. But I felt I got nothing out of it.

I then discovered a transvestite-transsexual support group which met every Saturday night in Upper Street, Islington. I remember the date – 10th December 1984 – as Liverpool was playing away to Chelsea, and I said I was going to Stamford Bridge. Instead I went to Lewisham and changed into a dress – size 12, I was quite thin – got a bus to Catford and did my hair in the Ladies. It felt like a blast from the past as it was the first time I had ventured out dressed as a girl for about 14 months.

I was less comfortable when I entered the meeting room of the transvestite-transsexual support group in a community centre on Upper Street. The door had been answered by a man in drag and I followed him into a hallway and down a short corridor into a well-lit room buzzing with conversation. The first thing I saw scared the life out of me. There were men in miniskirts with fishnet tights and forests of hair growing out through the holes in the tights. Tattooed lorry drivers sat with their legs spread wide apart and pint mugs of beer in front of them.

It was obviously a popular social club, but my first thought was that these people were freaks. I was sixteen and terrified that I looked similarly ludicrous. Do I look like that? I wondered. I was in shock and couldn't take it all in. I thought everyone looked grotesque. I did not relate to men in drag at all, and I didn't see anyone I could identify as a transsexual. There was absolutely nobody who appeared definitely, incontrovertibly womanly.

I sat and listened to a few of the men who were sharing their troubles. Everything was so depressing. So negative. Suddenly the doctor's ghastly prediction came rushing back to me.

I was introduced to another group who were more upbeat and interesting. I even confided that I needed to get a 'sex-change' operation but didn't know how. One of the men suggested I contact the Charing Cross Hospital Gender Identity Clinic and gave me the number. He looked like a gay man rather than a woman, but at least he seemed to know what he was talking about.

So the meeting had a good outcome. And as I was leaving to catch the bus home, around ten, one of the organisers of the evening approached me and asked for a word.

He led me upstairs to his office, fetched some coffee from a machine, and sat me down opposite him on a low chair.

'About that sex change,' he said. 'You don't want to do it. People make terrible mistakes. They think that changing their sex will put everything right – like their Fairy Godmother's descended and their problems are all going to vanish. But they're still the same person, it's just that now they've got medical problems as well. They've still got rent to pay, and they're damaged . It doesn't work.' He shook his head. 'How old are you?'

'Sixteen.'

'Oh my God! There's a big bloody – literally bloody – difference between what you're doing now and getting your whole engine taken out and replaced with something else. It's a huge, painful, horrible thing, and you're on tablets for years. I've known people who never get over it. You'll always regret it.'

'But I've always known I'm a girl.'

'I'm sure you have, but what you are talking about never works. Not properly. People end up with no feeling. They've got the works, but they don't have orgasms. They don't have jobs either. They have terrible mental distress and it does not end. You have seen some of them downstairs,' he added meaningfully.

He knew from my face that I'd met some truly sad people.

71

'But I can't go on like this. I can't live my whole life in the wrong body.'

'People do.'

He took me downstairs. As he opened the door he said: 'Really. Settle for what you've got and enjoy dressing up.'

'But I live with my parents!'

He sighed. 'Come round to my house if you want. Here's my number, you can come round and dress up whenever you want. Really. Call me.'

On the bus on the way home I sat on the top deck, staring out into the dark, with tears running down my face. I was upset for days. I kept the phone number where I'd written it, on my weekly bus ticket, for ages, but I never called him.

Instead I rang the Gender Identity Clinic. The woman who answered explained that I'd need a referral from a GP. My heart sank for an instant – but I could find another doctor.

'We'll look out for the letter. What's your name?' I gave it.

'And your date of birth?' I gave that, too.

'Oh, I'm sorry. You're too young. The doctors here can't see anyone until they're twenty-one.'

'Oh.' Her words felt like a thunderbolt straight into the middle of my being, I felt a lump in my throat and could hardly say goodbye. Could I wait? Five years seemed an eternity.

But I had no choice. I was trapped but knew I would never give up.

9 | IN THE SHADOW OF A NEW DEMON

Dad was now a couple of inches shorter than the six foot two inches tall he'd been before his fall from the balcony. I towered over him, but he still had the physical advantage. There was physical fear and I have always shrunk from violence. Flight, rather than fight, is my natural reaction. My brother was different. He was always the hardest boy in his year at school. He wouldn't have dared stand up to our father – that came later – but he was giving my parents grief, all the same; fighting and hanging out with local louts older than him. There were gang wars in Thamesmead and he'd started leaving the house at one in the morning. He had gone away to another school in the west of England, but he didn't fit in and mum and dad had to take days off work to go and see him. Now he was back at home, having effectively left school at fourteen.

My parents had no time to worry about me. They had my brother to think about, and money. The chip shop in Plumstead wasn't bringing in enough to pay the mortgage. They had to sell the house. They took over someone else's fish and chip shop in South Croydon which had a three-bedroom maisonette above.

I moved with them and struggled back and forth by bus from Selsdon to East Croydon, then by a series of trains to do my YTS course. The journey took about an hour-and-a-half each way. It was dispiriting. I stopped staying on in Woolwich for the A levels in the evenings.

Some nights I worked in the fish and chip shop after I got home. But some days that summer I took a very early morning bus to Wimbledon, and queued for a ground pass for the tennis. And if you queued at five in the afternoon, you could get a returned ticket for the Championships in the Centre Court or Number 1 Court. I did this several years in succession and saw all the stars – Chrissie Evert, Ivan Lendl, Martina Navratilova, Helena Sukova (who was nearly as tall as me) – and this year Boris Becker, who was my age and won the men's singles.

I read Martina Navratilova's autobiography and was fascinated by how she'd come to terms with her sexuality. It comforted me and gave me hope. My own life seemed to be all about waiting. I was clinging grimly to my mountainside, waiting for a helicopter, knowing that nothing I did would make it get here any faster.

On Tuesdays I was a regular at Fruit Machine at Heaven, the club under the arches at Charing Cross. I was trying to be a gay youth, though usually I appeared androgynous. Sometimes I adopted Madonna's look of the time: lace gloves, calf-length leggings, with a skirt under a little jacket. I could change in the single carriages between East Croydon and London Bridge. Rolling stock on the West Croydon line was being upgraded to long open-plan carriages, so if a modern train came in I would have to wait for the next one.

Some Saturdays, I'd be roaring from the terraces at Plough Lane. When I couldn't see Liverpool I adopted Wimbledon as my team; they'd been nowhere until the late 70s, not even in the League, but already they were in the second division. Other Saturdays, I wandered around in Top Shop or Camden Market, buying clothes or wishing I could afford them. But I noticed an ominous change at Heaven. I could see that while Annie Lennox and Boy George had appeared androgynous, which was very much my thing, the look was changing. Spandau Ballet and Duran Duran were all in smart suits and suddenly a lot of boys didn't seem to be wearing makeup any more. Androgyny was not exactly over yet, but going out of style.

More terrifyingly, AIDS had been identified. I noticed the cultural shift long before I recognised the cause.

Sometime in the summer of '85 AIDS, the understanding of it and its association mainly with gay men became mainstream. AIDS was terrifying: incurable. So are a lot of other diseases, but this, we were instructed, was a largely avoidable infection. Be celibate, never use needles, never get a blood transfusion, and you'd be unlikely to die of it. As Rock Hudson did. Terence Higgins collapsed in Heaven. The red-tops called it the Gay Plague. Have you shared a cup with a gay person? My dad took his own glass to the pub.

Some said 'oh it's just the press trying to wind us up.' But three people I knew died of it. In late 1985 I had an HIV test and the result was negative. But when you had the second test three months later it was still only an MOT for the date you had first been tested. There was never any guarantee. So I adjusted my practices accordingly. You didn't always know if you'd got the virus, but it allowed you to catch other, terrible diseases. People as young as twenty lost all their fat and muscle, and tottered about like walking skeletons. Others just died. The Government commissioned a campaign that autumn. There was the TV ad, with an iceberg, and threatening music, and a warning to be vigilant. A leaflet came through every front door: AIDS: DON'T DIE OF IGNORANCE. In terms of public education, it led the world – urging acceptance of the facts, without being morbid, prurient or judgmental.

Gay-bashing had been around forever but it was making headlines now. And one summer night, after catching the night bus home after I'd been to the Fridge, in Brixton Hill, it happened to me.

My bus had stopped short of my destination and I was at the bus stop waiting for the next one when three youths came along. They were about seventeen. A few cars had sped by in the dark. It was late, and for London, quiet. 'Fucking queer', one said. 'Aids-carrier' yelled another, before he spat on me and punched me, knocking me against a wall before a bus bore down on us and they ran off.

By the time I got home everyone else had gone to bed, so I quietly sneaked into the bathroom to examine my injuries. I had bruised ribs and cuts, and my face was sore, with a livid bruise on my right cheekbone and a fiery graze, oozing blood, from jaw to chin. That wasn't going to disappear overnight.

I washed the blood off and went to bed. But in the morning I had to face mum in the kitchen.

'Jeez what happened to you?'

'I got mugged.'

'Oh my god. The blackguards! Why didn't you wake your dad up?'

'It was at a bus stop in Streatham, mum.'

'Did they get anything? Who were they? How many of them?'

'Two – I didn't see them properly. They hit me and I fell over and hit my face on the kerb, then they said give us your money so I did and they ran off.'

'Did you fetch the police?'

'Yeah, I went down and gave a description. I don't think they'll do anything. It was dark and it was so quick – I didn't see their faces.'

'Were there no witnesses?'

'There was nobody about. Just cars going past.'

Of course I hadn't reported it. It was well known that if you did you might get beaten up by the police as well. In Small Town Boy, the video, Jimmy Somerville gets gay-bashed. A policeman brings him home and explains the situation precisely. The father goes to attack him; the policeman intervenes. Next day the boy is thrown out of the house.

Such experiences left me feeling more vulnerable, isolated and alienated from ordinary society. The song, a real anthem for being different, says 'never cry to them but to your soul'. My soul was fast becoming all cried out. My body, in the latter stages of puberty, repulsed me. I could never look in a mirror naked.

When the YTS course finally came to an end, I applied for a job as a payroll clerk in Croydon and was invited to an interview. I got my hair cut and styled and wore a suit. After our discussion, Mrs Kaye, the office manager, probably expecting to find me at home, phoned up and spoke to my dad. She told him I'd got the job and how impressed she had been by my maturity of outlook.

He told me this with an air of disbelief. His first-born son had got what he regarded as a woman's job. In his world, men got real jobs, physical ones. Driving, or even a trade.

As for me, hallelujah, I'd got a nine-to-five, Monday to Friday job at a decent rate of pay. I was a junior payroll clerk only a bus ride from where we lived. I liked it. It was a company that supplied payroll services to Marks and Spencer, and of a workforce of twenty only three of us were men. I shared an office with four women, all much older than me, which I found slightly intimidating.

Meanwhile the AIDS ad campaign was everywhere and I decided that if I was going to be gay for the next five years – till I could change my gender – I wouldn't be quite so visibly 'out'. I kept quiet, worked hard, stopped going to clubs and stopped dressing up. I decided to save up, get a flat and better clothes and compensate by going to more football.

By Christmas 1985, I had been a diligent employee for several months. I was saving money. My parents had sold the house, cleared their debts and were buying a new, cheaper property in Gillingham. Completion would take place late in January.

I was glad for them but didn't think it affected me. I could afford at least a bedsit now, so I'd stay in Croydon. I certainly wasn't about to live in Gillingham; it was miles east of London, in Kent.

In the new year Mrs Kaye made an announcement. The company was going to relocate to Slough, far beyond west London, with effect from next month.

10 | MY POLITICAL AWAKENING

Within days of losing my job, I woke up living in Gillingham, thirty-five miles from Charing Cross, a town where people moved in slow motion, and the only jobs available were local and low-paid.

If you are a person who has never been poor, and like Norman Tebbit believes that everyone in that situation should 'get on their bike', you are possibly right. Unfortunately certain obstacles stand in the way.

Number one: I didn't have a bike. Or a car, or money to run one, though I'd passed my driving test.

Number two: the jobs that I could do, that paid a decent wage, were always advertised in the London Evening Standard. The paper was not on sale in Gillingham, but appeared on London streets from about 1pm. Anybody who was at a City newsstand, with money for a payphone to make calls, would be first off the starting block. A daily return ticket into town was not within my means.

Number three: if I got the first full-time job that came up – running a public toilet, for instance – I wouldn't have unemployment benefit, so I'd be exactly where I was now, without the advantage of spare time in which to apply to do something better. If I got a part-time McJob I'd also be no better off financially (the Government reduced your benefit for every hour you worked) and again, I'd have less time.

There may have been a practical solution, but without money, most avenues of opportunity close down. Your one smart suit needs dry cleaning; you've just grown out of another pair of shoes (I was now six foot five with size 10 feet, and still growing). Even time wasn't always free. In those days you had to queue in the employment exchange and queue again in the Post Office to get your money. If you had a relentlessly sunny disposition and the all-conquering confidence of a young Richard Branson, I suppose you'd get up at three in the morning and walk 35 miles into the City to go to interviews in trainers. But being poor makes you feel inadequate and saps your energy.

Ours was a small Edwardian house near the station. At this time it wasn't a happy house. The older of my two sisters, who was about fourteen, slammed doors and rowed with mum and dad and couldn't wait to leave school. My brother was away somewhere, but he was a worry. Dad was doing some mini-cabbing and getting relief work managing fish and chip shops.

I signed on. I went to the library. I wrote applications. I made phone calls. I watched television. At this rate dad's grumbles would force me into a McJob in the end. I began applying for office jobs locally. I tried hard not to get into a rut but found myself watching the ITV News at the same time every day. From the week before we left Croydon, it had been all about the Wapping dispute.

Rupert Murdoch's News International, which produced The Times among other papers, had left Fleet Street for new, state-of-the-art offices in Wapping. Journalists would input the stories directly, by electronic means; printing would be digital and highly automated; production would be vastly quicker. Thousands of hot-lead Linotype typesetters and compositors, all highly skilled men, would be redundant.

Strikers with banners picketed the Wapping site. The television broadcast scenes of violent disorder. Policemen with riot shields, some of them on horseback, bore down with visible brutality. Local people reported being treated like criminals. Murdoch's papers reported that strikers had thrown pennies under the horses' hooves to make them slip on the cobbles. There was pain and tenacity on both sides.

The NUJ's objections were nothing by comparison with the printers'. One of our uncles-by-marriage was a Fleet Street printer. Printers were at the very top of the working-class financial tree. They'd traditionally been on good money with jobs for life and jobs for their sons, too. Until Rupert Murdoch came along.

The main print union, SOGAT, was a closed shop, as most of the big unions were, then. This meant that you couldn't work 'in the print' unless you were in the union, and you couldn't join the union unless four printers recommended you as professionally competent (which they couldn't because you couldn't work unless you were in the union). It matched prestigious clubs like White's or the Athenaeum for exclusivity, and once you were in the fierce class loyalty was similar as well. And the News International printers were men, although some union members from allied trades were women. Their General Secretary, surprisingly in a male-dominated union, was Brenda Dean.

In the past, the newspaper proprietors had always conceded to SOGAT. It wasn't worth fighting – one day's strike, and your readers would flit to another paper and probably not return. But Murdoch had the financial clout to implement a strategic business decision. It made sense to computerise the expensive labour-intensive print process. And behind him was Margaret Thatcher. She saw that this was a key confrontation that must take place if Britain was to move forward into the world of new technology.

Her Government's policy since 1979 had been to shift the emphasis of Britain's economy away from primary and manufacturing industries because she believed we couldn't compete globally in those. Our labour costs were too high, our domestic customer base too small. In pursuit of this policy, the miners had already been defeated after months of strikes and most mines closed down as 'uneconomic' to run. The coalfields of Britain had become the idealogical battlefield where unions and Thatcherism fought . Not for the first or last time had the working class been let down by those who purported to represent them. Mrs Thatcher knew how to pick her enemies and she couldn't have dreamed of a better opponent than Arthur Scargill. The result was a raft of social misery and critics of Thatcher never forgave her. At the same time London's docks were shut, Midlands car manufacturers were dying, and shipbuilders in the Northern ports were struggling.

From now on, we were told, this small island would concentrate on services. But the service industries had to slim down in preparation for a bright new technologically-advanced dawn. Banking and trading would change, that summer of '86, when regulations were relaxed in the Big Bang. Bank messengers who had carried information across the City for longer than anyone could remember, traders yelling on the Stock Exchange floor, complacent boardrooms where a few City families had provided generations of Chairmen, would vanish.

Back office work was changing. In accounts departments since before the war, there had been lady comptometer operators. They were rare now, replaced with people like me who knew a bit about information technology and whose computers, usually connected to a big mainframe, did the sums faster and more reliably. In fashionable offices people were using early Apple Mac computers and at home they had Amstrads with green screens. People had started to use ATMs instead of queuing for money at a bank counter; in shops, credit card payments could already be made via terminals connected to vast computer centres hundreds of miles away.

Every night on the TV news a big beast of mass communication was slowly gaining the upper hand. I supported the Government's position, and by extension, Murdoch's. But where exactly I would fit in to this contest between labour and capital, if at all, I wasn't sure.

After about three weeks I got a dull job in Gillingham, in stock control. But I didn't care if it was boring. I reasoned that I would be adrift in this small town until I was twenty one; the job filled my days, paid the rent and left me with just enough money to get into London for fun. I stuck with it for about ten months.

Between mini-cabbing, dad relief-managed fish and chip shops. He was running one near Baker Street, so on Saturday mornings he would give me a lift. Going out dressed as a girl was getting more important to me, but I had to plan it all in advance. I'd get a lift into London with dad, then dump my bag of clothes and makeup in Left Luggage at Charing Cross. Personally operated left-luggage lockers still existed, which was surprising since London was still under threat of bombing by the IRA.

I'd shop, go to a football match, see friends from a group in the evening, then collect my bag and change into a dress, sometimes on the train into town. Because my locker would be inaccessible in the middle of the night, I had to take my bag of male clothes with me to Heaven. I'd check it in at the cloakroom, pick it up on my way out, and get back to Gillingham, having changed back into my dull alter-ego on the paper train.

I met and saw the most surprising people at Heaven. Even their everyday lives seemed to belong in a world a million miles from mine: judges, barristers, doctors – Sam Fox the Page Three girl was well known and often there, although she hadn't come out as gay at the time. I was asked back to parties. I was in the kitchen of somebody's gothic house when a pasty-faced man with lots of eyeshadow walked in, stopped dead and said: 'Who are you?' I told him and he sauntered away again. It was Boy George, and I was at his house, at his party. It was my only encounter with this icon of my generation. He'd always maintained an unbelievably clean image, but he was arrested soon afterwards when somebody overdosed and died in that house.

I was always wary of drugs, and not just because I didn't know much about them. I couldn't afford to lose control. Everything was so delicately balanced in my life; the whole edifice could have crashed down.

I caught the last train to London every Tuesday night and occasionally dressed up on the journey. I always got back in time for work on Wednesday morning, looking sober and committed. In my employment contract there was something about male employees having to have short hair, no earring, and 'appropriate clothing.' That would be a suit, shirt and tie, then.

It was good training for a life of serial infidelity or espionage. I planned every tiny detail that might give me away.

One night I went back to the Upper Street transsexual group. It had moved to Shoreditch, and was better. Or perhaps it was that at eighteen I was more realistic and accepting of others. I now saw transsexual females who would have blended in anywhere. Maybe, because I had been so stunned with shock on my first visit, I simply hadn't noticed them last time.

I liked the people but I couldn't relate to them. Even today I don't have transsexual friends. We were introduced, it was sociable and everybody was nice. But I didn't feel I fitted in. I couldn't simply tell them that I was a girl in the wrong body. The gay community can be very compartmentalised and even bigoted. Gay men and lesbians often sneer at each other, bisexuals are mistrusted, and nobody knows what to make of 'transgendered' individuals. Not even themselves, quite often.

Everybody else at that group felt it was a lifesaver, a place where they could reveal their true selves. Not me. I did try – I even went to a drag ball at the Porchester Hall. But it wasn't an experience I'd ever want to repeat; I felt out of place. I felt nothing in common with these people. I was still leading a double life.

After Christmas I got a job at Lloyd's Black Horse Life in Chatham, close to Gillingham but a more interesting place. It did at least boast historical associations with Dickens and the Navy, and had a tourist trade, better shops and a sense of connection to the world that Gillingham always lacked. Like Woolwich, Chatham was a squaddie town and had barracks.

There was also a huge and growing property bubble and some of the big five banks, as they then were, had bought chains of estate agents. Lloyd's owned Black Horse. Before people could get a mortgage they had to satisfy the mortgage company that they had life insurance which would cover them for the duration of the loan. Lloyd's could provide that life insurance. Underwriters, guided by actuarial data on their computers, assessed an applicant's chances of survival for however many years, and made the decision. Applicants who got turned down or didn't hear anything generally rang their local branch of Lloyd's to ask about it, and the branch would call Chatham and discuss their case. I began as a junior grade 0, hunting for people's files, but within a year I was grade 4 and a Liaison Officer, taking queries from branches and discussing them with the underwriters.

I liked it. At eighteen, when your social and sexual life is incredibly important, a nine-to-five job in which you are learning and getting regular pay rises is terrific. With dad's help, I bought a car. I went to gay bars, and had relationships with men that lasted a few weeks or months. I was young so I didn't have to buy my own drinks. I was popular, I knew people, there was a bit of a community, and I was having fun.

And I had another passion: the General Election in June, 1987. I did loads of work for the Gillingham Conservatives in the evenings. They were well-to-do, middle-class people, who welcomed me as a Party member. And why wouldn't they? I was an upwardly mobile Young Conservative who made it plain that I detested the Labour party for betraying the working class. I delivered thousands and thousands of leaflets, knocked on doors – dad practically sweated exasperation. He couldn't believe I was really a Conservative. It made no sense to him.

He reserved a particularly dismissive tone for Denis Thatcher. 'Big streak o'nothing,' dad barked, whenever Denis, with his 'goofy' grin, appeared on TV, lurking alongside Maggie. 'Never done an honest day's work in his life!' 'Trails after her...' He couldn't adjust to the role reversal in that household. As for Denis having been a war hero, self-made millionaire and director of a multi-national oil company – Prrhh. War hero, he'd probably been in the Stores... the other two were not proper jobs.

Neil Kinnock was the Labour leader now; a ginger-haired fellow bursting with bonhomie, but usually referred to as the 'Welsh Windbag' in my political circle. His party looked like a threat to some who doubted Maggie. Not to me. On the night, the count was held at the Sports Centre in Gillingham. The result was declared at about one in the morning, with our candidate, a nice but uncontroversial MP, winning a big majority.

After the congratulations, half a glass of Prosecco and the speeches, I sped down to Smith Square in my Austin Allegro. I parked on Millbank, picked a path through dozens of outside-broadcast vans, arc lights, reporters and cables trailing across the tarmac around St John's, Smith Square and there, above me, were Maggie and Norman Tebbit, smiling from a brilliantly-lit upper window of the Tory Party HQ on the corner. There was a big party going on inside.

Her 144-seat majority was cut, but not significantly. It was all about adoring Maggie, rather than the Party's policies, at that time. People who'd never aspired to own houses were buying them. Money was cheap, credit more available than ever. The south-east seemed afloat on a tide of consumer spending.

I occasionally went up to Liverpool for football matches, and saw a different world of grey deprivation. I blamed Labour for that; their administration of Liverpool City Council was notoriously corrupt, and the party in Westminster seemed powerless to control infiltration in the provinces by their far-left Militant tendency.

Maggie took on the Labour councils as she'd taken on the Trade Unions. She dissolved the Greater London Council. I thought it was good riddance. Ken Livingstone's 'London – Nuclear Free Zone!' campaign had struck me as a particularly annoying waste of taxpayers' money. But when he hung anti-Thatcher banners on the outside of City Hall, right across the river from the Houses of Parliament, he was toast.

I got promoted for a third, and – later that summer – a fourth time. I was popular at the office, where my job involved lots of interaction with people. I was friends with many of the underwriters – most of them worked in a different part of the building – but since my job meant consulting them about why a person had been turned down for life assurance and what they could do about it, I talked to them on the phone all day long. That meant gossip about girlfriends and boyfriends, and what they'd done at the weekend, the assumption being that I was heterosexual and so, of course, were they. I talked about football matches at the weekend. I suppose because I seemed to be unattached girls began to hang around. Embarrassed, I invented fictitious girlfriends. It was stressful, because this new pack of lies was just one more complication in what should have been a fairly straightforward existence.

Thanks to Pride, which was then called Gay Pride, the solution arrived. At that summer's Pride I ran into a girl from the office. She was a lesbian, and assumed that I was a gay man. From then on, as we both worked on the eighth floor ,we became 'openly' friendly and everyone else decided we were an item.

I looked good. My greasy hair and spots had gone. I had left home and rented my own small flat in Chatham. I also had a personal life. I was seeing, semi-seriously, a man called Stuart. At thirty-eight he was exactly twice my age. That didn't separate us so much as his earning capacity, which was in many multiples of mine. He worked in the City and these were the boom years. He was also firmly in the closet.

We'd met in a bar. He lived in Pimlico and had a villa in Spain. We spent many weeks of that summer there, and weekends too. The office ran on flexitime, and people would cover for you if you got in at 11am on Mondays. It was a friendly office, with no in-fighting.

Everything was falling into place. I felt independent. I adored being in Spain, going to football, parties, everything. I felt optimistic about the future; when everything's going well, it seems everything always will. I told Stuart what I intended to do when I was twenty-one and he was okay about it, although in a cautious 'Okay For Now' kind of way. He was seeing me, and understandably found it difficult to come to terms with the idea that the person who was me might, one day, be a girl.

I occasionally went into Westminster Cathedral for a quiet minute, when I was in Pimlico at weekends. I am not a lapsed Catholic, even now, and at that point I was more of a gently subsiding one. I never went to churches of other denominations. I still enjoyed helping out with the handicapped children's charity, paying for myself to go to Lourdes with the kids every year and raising money for them. But I stopped going to church every Sunday because I finally allowed myself to admit that I was conflicted. On the one hand, the Church's teachings; on the other, my private life.

If I'd been what the media still, nearly thirty years later, call openly gay, I might have felt less concern. But in an office like mine that was out of the question. I was a troubleshooter. Part of my job was to ask why an application had been 'loaded' by a certain number of points. Usually it was a history of serious illness or the fact that someone had a perilous occupation like being a steeplejack or a lion tamer. But now there was a new questionnaire directed only at single men. Are you a homosexual? Are you bisexual? Have you ever had intercourse with a prostitute? Have you ever taken intravenous drugs? Have you ever had an HIV test? If you answered yes to any of these, even if you'd had a negative HIV test, your policy would be heavily loaded. You could of course lie, but your life insurance would be invalidated if you did, and died of AIDS.

I was constantly reminded that by inflicting conformity, you make people unhappy. So I rationalised my feelings around Catholicism. I thought the Ten Commandments are about honouring your father and your mother, keeping the Sabbath holy, not ogling other people's chattels and never killing anybody. But not one of them is about homosexuality. If I do my best out of the ten, I told myself, I'll be Ok. I don't steal things, and I'll try about the Sabbath.

The hardest thing was not coveting other people's chattels. Stuart was big on chattels. He had a Filofax (I had one too) and a state-of-the-art mobile phone that worked off a charger the size and weight of a house-brick. I wanted one of those, desperately.

11 | AN ENDING AND A NEW BEGINNING

The fling with Stuart ended in early 1988. I was disappointed, but not bereft. Endings are nature's way of giving you opportunities for review and progress and the disappointment was nothing compared to my ongoing gender identity crisis. I was still eighteen months away from any chance of an appointment at the clinic, so I started talking with my brother about what we were both going to do next. I wanted to go to America. He needed a job first, to get some money together. He'd got a motor mechanic's qualification, but in the end he joined the army. He was six foot five and the Army put him into the Queen's Guard.

I had another friend who was keen to go America with me, so I worked on at Lloyds, saving money, and planned to leave in September. But the friend dropped out at the last moment, by which time I'd saved £1,200, given notice at my job and my flat, and had bought, for £256, an Icelandair return ticket to New York, valid for a year.

When the plane took off, and I was staring down at the steaming tarmac of Heathrow, I wondered whether I'd ever come back. I planned to live in hostels and find casual work when I got there. Almost anything seemed possible, and I hoped that somehow I might be able to get the gender-change operation more easily in the States.

In Reykjavik, waiting for my connecting flight, I hooked up with an English couple and we all ended up at the same hostel in Times Square. This was before Giuliani cleaned up New York: there were trannie prostitutes, drug dealers offering cocaine on the street corner, guns in evidence, and screaming police car chases that gave the night-time streets more than a passing resemblance to an episode of Starsky and Hutch. The subway was full of scary people and some of the stations stank. If I hadn't been with others I think I would have left

89

New York within twelve hours. As it was I stayed several days and when we'd done the usual Manhattan tourist trail I got a $70 flight to Los Angeles.

I found a hostel in Huntington Beach that cost $65 a week and started to earn double that in cash, cleaning and sanding boats and serving in a little burger bar with a view of the ocean. I worked sixteen hours a week and for the rest of my time I was free to be a beach bum.

I let my hair grow long and looked around. You could get a bus through South Central LA and into the more glamorous Sunset Boulevard and Hollywood regions, so I did. But I was wary of looking for work there. I now knew – having initially been unbelievably naïve about this when I left England – that as an alien, though legally in the country, I was prohibited from doing paid work without a social security number. And I'd be in big trouble if I got caught.

'You can marry somebody,' an English guy in the hostel told me. I had been living there for months by then and I loved it. We were in the kitchen and a few of us were cooking while others sat at the table. 'Then you can get a green card.' Everybody agreed that English guys were popular.

But I didn't need more complications. Marriage for me had a religious significance. Also, I had read about, and by now had met, people who had been married with children before they changed sex and I found their situation hard to grasp. Apparently there is such a thing as late-onset gender conflict, but I couldn't come to terms with it on any level that made sense to me. I'd known who I was since I was a kid, and the whole idea that a person could wake up when they were forty... Besides, if a married man turned into a woman, and kept on living with his wife, what was going on there? Did she become a lesbian? For me it was like running through a hall of mirrors.

Though I absolutely loved Californian optimism and the sunshine, with only weeks to go to Christmas, I started missing my family. And football. I'd seen Liverpool, the top team in all Europe, lose to

Wimbledon – Wimbledon! – in the Cup Final that year. They missed a penalty. I was pleased for Wimbledon, of course, but I would never forget the physical sensation of my heart sinking through my feet into the concrete at the penalty miss by John Aldridge.

I had bought a Liverpool season ticket before I left for America. It had cost me a hard-earned £60 and I wasn't using it. Why didn't I go home for a month and then come back?

Nothing had changed in Gillingham. In January there was not only rain, but it was bitterly cold. To make matters worse I had to stay with my parents.

I signed on and started looking for work. But within the first few weeks I'd had enough, swallowed my pride and went back to my old job. At the back of my mind I was counting the days. Only six months to go now and I'd be twenty-one and able to get a referral letter to a gender clinic.

My brother was at home too. He'd been invalided out of the Army after a bad leg injury made him permanently unfit. He wasn't much bothered about leaving, he had matured a lot, and knew now that he needed to persist and find the job he really wanted as a mechanic.

Playing football had got him into this mess. He'd twisted, fallen and smashed his thigh as someone fell on top of him. He was an Arsenal supporter but we drove up to Liverpool games together. I had a Kop season ticket, the Kop being the main standing area at Liverpool's Anfield ground behind the goal.

One of the matches I went to that spring – without him – was an FA Cup semi-final between Liverpool and Nottingham Forest. FA Cup games are played on neutral territory and this one was to be in Sheffield, at the Hillsborough ground, on 15th April.

Normally when you bought tickets for away games you'd be given the equivalent of your home season ticket entitlement at the away stadium. This at Hillsborough was also called the Kop and was at the east end of the pitch. The west end, Leppings Lane, had less room and only about a third of the turnstiles. It would have made sense to give Liverpool fans the Kop end plus the south stands, because Liverpool were well supported and Nottingham Forest were not. In fact the smaller Nottingham contingent were assigned the Kop, on police advice, because they would come and go from that end.

When the terraces were full, Liverpool fans were put in standing room at the tighter Leppings Lane end. The police had one aim: containment. Any lip, and you'd get arrested in a heartbeat. In the eighties that's the way football matches were – for the away team especially. At Anfield, our home ground, we were invincible. The Kop was legendary; the sense of belonging, of shared passion, was exhilerating. I loved every single minute of it. When tens of thousands of us sang 'You'll Never Walk Alone' we did it with pride.

Football had a bad side. At away matches it was common to be pelted with coins or broken glass, or be urinated on from the stands above. And the police could be vicious. They were quick to hit out with their truncheons. If you went to football matches at the time you were not surprised by violence.

At Hillsborough I had a seat ticket, thanks to a friend who hadn't been able to go, in the north stand. I'd been to this ground the year before and there had been a visible cordon of uniforms to get through, with police scrutinising every ticket. This time that didn't happen and it seemed to be a bit of a free-for-all. Kick-off was at 3pm but great waves of people were still coming in to the Leppings Lane end after 2.45.

The atmosphere was building in the way it always did at Liverpool games in the days of Kenny Dalglish's reign. We were Kenny's Army. And we were on our way to Wembley. The roar of anticipation was loudest from behind the goal. The pens on either side were not very full, but it looked as if thousands were still pouring in to the central pen.

It was a shambles down there, but I didn't know that. A lot of Liverpool supporters had been delayed by road works as they drove across the Pennines, and arrived late. The police had kept the main gate open until the last minute but failed to block off the tunnel to the central pens behind the goal, which were already overflowing. And with thousands of people still pouring in when the match started the ones in front were pushed right up against the soaring steel fences that penned the standing spectators behind the goal and the pitch.

But I'd stopped looking – the match had begun. I only noticed something amiss a few minutes in when a few people from behind the wire at our end had somehow got onto the pitch and the police were trying to push them back. But they kept coming. The police looked as if they hadn't got control and were unsure what to do. People began to struggle through a break in the fence and others were clambering up out of the crowd and being hauled up and over the barrier fronting the stand above. Police were at the fence now, but I couldn't see what they were doing.

I felt dismayed. You see what you expect to see and it looked like crowd trouble. Four years before at Heysel in Belgium, thirty-nine Italian fans had been killed when 'Liverpool fans' rampaged (though who they really were is still disputed; National Front cells managed to infiltrate a lot of clubs in the eighties). We had a reputation. It looked as if Liverpool supporters were trying to rush the pitch now and the police were pushing them back.

Six minutes in the ref stopped the match. Figures in their hundreds swarmed over the pitch and ran out of control around the fence, part of which was sagging. The roar of voices deafened me; spectators were saying that people had been killed but nobody knew. I saw two or three ambulances driving onto the grass, hoardings being ripped down and used as stretchers.

We were told to evacuate the stadium and shuffled out in our thousands to the sound of sirens. The match was being broadcast and I thought of my parents, who might just hear something alarming on the radio. I looked for a phone box but the queues were already miles long. I heard people shouting angrily, blaming the police, and saw one or two whose little transistor radios were broadcasting a commentary which didn't enlighten me. Some people were desperately shouting the names of their kids or mums and dads – the police were no help at all. All people wanted to do was find their families, but police officers were officious, relentlessly bullying the frantic people trying to get out.

I got into my car, which crawled away in the chaos of departing traffic and incoming ambulances, and called my mum from a phone box at the first service station on the motorway to tell her I was OK. I listened to the radio on the way home, broadcasting direct from the ground. Forty, then sixty-three, then over seventy people had been pronounced dead, and by the time I got home it was over eighty. All these deaths were attributed to crushing: asphyxiation under the press of bodies, or against that steel fence. There were small boys in there, and grandmothers, and whole families. Two teenage sisters had been lost. On Match of the Day that night they didn't show any football, just pictures of what had happened.

The immediate outcome of that match was ninety-five people dead. The following week my brother and I drove up to Anfield to add our own bouquet to the carpet of flowers covering the pitch.

Tony Bland, aged eighteen, was brain-damaged and in a coma or four more years until his life support was turned off, making him the ninety-sixth victim. In answer to all the enquiries that followed the Hillsborough disaster, police at every level lied shamelessly. They blamed Liverpool supporters.

They were not held to account for nearly a quarter of a century, when their statements were officially said to have perverted the course of justice. Resentment is still raw: Justice for the ninety-six is our demand. Like most Liverpool supporters I want to see Chief Superintendent Duckenfield, whose negligence was ultimately responsible, charged with manslaughter. Deaths by compression against crowd control barriers had happened before at British football grounds, notably at Ibrox Park in '71. All the organisers should have been aware and the police in particular. British grounds have become seat-only as a result of Hillsborough and must stay that way; I can think of ninety-six reasons why.

Hillsborough still matters to me because of my own guilt at my first instinct – utterly and tragically wrong – that the overcrowding was somehow the result of the fans. It is one of my most personal experiences of deadly injustice. And I still boil and rage at anyone who dares question what is now accepted as the truth.

I left Lloyd's out of boredom, in the end, and became a trainee manager at Gateway supermarket. Did I have a sudden urge to price cat food and discuss Eastenders in the canteen with checkout ladies twice my age? No I did not. But I was still drifting and did it for the sake of doing something different. I was still living at home, miles from London. On days when I felt depressed I reflected that I'd moved backwards. California had been great and I'd meant to return almost at once. But I never did.

My birthday arrived at last. I went to a new doctor, in Gillingham. And this time I was determined to be assertive. If the doctor refused to consider my request, I would ask for a second opinion. However, he didn't. He referred me to the Gender Identity Clinic at Charing Cross Hospital and a week later they sent me a letter. The first available appointment would be Monday 31st January 1990, with consultant psychiatrist Dr Hohberger.

I had begun, late that summer, going to Liverpool and staying on after matches to go clubbing there. I was tired of Heaven. I didn't fit in there any more. Gay bars and clubs were getting fashionable with heterosexuals and I rarely saw anyone I knew. I been to Liverpool so many times now that I'd begun to feel some affection for the place. It had a horrible traffic system, but there were brilliant old hilly streets in the middle, lively pubs and clubs and a spectacular waterside. You could see from the massive Victorian buildings how rich it had once been.

So I drove all the way to Liverpool at weekends to distract myself from a directionless working life in which I turned up every day at Gateway and obediently got through training which wouldn't have taxed a twelve-year-old.

In September 1989, fidgeting, I decided to live up there. I applied for a transfer to a Gateway store in the north-west, and kept on marking time. If they refused I'd get a different job, because there was nothing for me here. They didn't refuse, even though I'd once committed the cardinal sin of forgetting to order baked beans for weekend.. (I never did live that down.)

At the end of January 1990, I knew that two months hence I'd be an Assistant Manager at a Gateway in the Wirral.

All that was on my mind however, was the appointment at Charing Cross. At last my aim was within sight.

12 | THE JOURNEY BEGINS

Charing Cross Hospital is one of the many places in London that is no longer where its name might suggest. Around the time I was born, it had moved a few miles west of Charing Cross to new buildings on the Fulham Palace Road.

But at the end of January, 1990, I had no trouble finding the Gender Identity Clinic for my meeting with Dr Hohberger. It was an appointment that had the power to change my life.

I had been told I could come dressed as I wished and had chosen a long green skirt and a black blouse. I felt apprehensive, but happy. By this time I had read books about the process of changing sex and I didn't think I would be let down again. There was no reason this would not be right for me.

Dr Hohberger had been working in this field for a long time. He was balding, in his fifties or sixties, pleasant and kind. He checked my date of birth and other personal details. Then he put down his pen.

'So tell me, what do you want? Why are you here?'

I felt as if a blockage in me had suddenly been released. I told him how I had felt all these years: that inside I had always known I was female and trapped in the wrong body; that all my ambitions were on hold until I felt 'right'. 'Surely,' I added, almost as a plea, 'you are the gender you feel you are?'

He said nothing but asked a lot more questions. Did I get sexual excitement from wearing women's clothes? No. He wanted to know my childhood thoughts and asked about my relationship with my parents. Then he asked: 'What does it feel like to be a woman?' I stumbled and paused. How could I answer that? It was simply about being me.

Dr Hohberger made no comment as he scribbled notes of my answers. I had been afraid that he might turn me away as a kind of neurotic attention-seeker for whom nobody else exists. He didn't. He took me very seriously, and I trusted him.

He did not inform me with the indulgent air of the Thamesmead doctor that I'd 'grow out of it' (which was just as well as I was now six foot five inches tall.) Nor did he patronise me by saying 'it's going to be OK', or 'it's going to be painless'. He was realistic and described with calm precision the physical and mental agony that gender change involves and the time it would take. He showed me diagrams detailing the surgery that would be required and explained what could go wrong. This was not cosmetic surgery. It was complete internal reconstruction, accompanied by a hormone replacement program that I'd probably endure for the rest of my life. The hormones alone could have some dangerous side-effects. I didn't care what they were. Being myself was what mattered.

Nor, at that first meeting, did he promise to arrange my surgery.

'I see myself as a kind of gatekeeper,' he said. 'By coming here you've reached the gate. On the other side are risk and pain, as well as a potentially promising future. You may tell me you want to pass through that gate, but I want you to spend the next three months thinking seriously about alternatives.

'Now that I have told you the facts, I hope you won't be too dismissive of those alternatives. Or any others you may already have considered. At this point nothing is lost. Nothing. You can walk out of here and lead a gay life or a straight one, as a man.

'You're suffering from gender dysphoria. If you choose simply to live your life as a woman with no physical intervention at all, I can supply you with a note that identifies your condition to anyone who thinks you're doing something outrageous – going into women's toilets, for instance. But if you decide to pass through the gate, you will start on a long path to becoming a different person entirely. Think about what you could lose by becoming that person, as well as what you can gain.'

'What happens if I come back and say I want to carry on?'

'Then the work really starts. You'll have to satisfy both of us that you can carry this through. You'll take the Harry Benjamin Pathway. Harry Benjamin was an American doctor, a specialist in gender dysphoria, and his Pathway is designed to give you every chance to reverse your decision if you want to, or alternatively ease you into a change of gender. But let's wait and see, shall we?'

I left his office with a certificate, signed by Dr Hohberger, that I could produce if ever I needed to. It identified me as a person who was gender dysphoric and undergoing treatment at Charing Cross Hospital and made it clear that I would be dressing as a woman, the gender I believed myself to be.

I felt overwhelming relief and happiness. I was on my way; and best of all, I felt vindicated. What I had was a recognised condition. And now I had been offered a way to sort it out.

I took his advice, and asked myself a lot of questions while I waited for my next appointment at the end of April. I'm not physically fearless like my brother but I knew I could face the pain. I knew that the hormones I would have to take to change my secondary sexual characteristics could make a person moody, but I was prepared for that. I couldn't wait to start.

I had no significant doubt about the way forward. I had never, as a gay man or as a boy, felt at ease. My gender was wrong. I wanted it put right and always had.

When I went back to give him my decision, he wasn't surprised.

'There is one thing, I said. 'You know I said I was moving to Liverpool. Well I have, so I'm going to need the letter for the consultant.'

He gave me the name of the man I'd be seeing.

I took the form he gave me and started filling it in with my address. 'Can you tell me when I'll have to start taking hormone tablets?'

'I don't prescribe them 'till much later,' he said. 'I like to see my patients firmly established on the Pathway before they take that step. The Pathway is the 'real life test.' But I'll talk about it to your doctor. It's normal for more than one of us to make decisions in cases like yours.'

In order to start on the Pathway, I would need to get a job as a woman – not immediately, but soon. I remembered what that gay man had told me years ago at the Islington transsexual meeting about how having the surgery too soon could have disastrous psychological results. The physical ones weren't necessarily very pretty either. It was a process that needed to go slowly and I understood that.

It is all too easy to fall overboard for a vision of ourselves, the way we fall in love with a person or crave a new car. If the vision, like the lover or the Porsche, turns out to have serious drawbacks, it can be a struggle to admit it; you've invested too much of your identity in the hoped-for outcome and may feel compelled to carry on, suppressing your remorse.

So I would need to live as a woman for a couple of years. Because of the P60s, P45s and all the other paperwork including a passport, I would need practical advice on changing my identity. Dr Hohberger told me that could be arranged later. I would also change my name.

For some reason from the age of 10 or 11 the names Nikki, Nicola or Nicole had resonated in my head. I don't know where I got them from. I had no relatives or friends with those names, nor was there any celebrity around that time called anything like that. I chose the Sinclaire by flicking through the telephone directory and stabbing a pen into the pages. I put an 'e' on the end of both Nicole and Sinclaire as it conformed to my notion of symmetry.

Up in Liverpool I'd begun a new relationship with a man I'd met in a club where I'd gone as a woman. When I started work up north I moved into his flat in Toxteth – in those days Liverpool's answer to Brixton. He was bisexual and said he understood my situation. So I hadn't just caught up with almost everything that had had to be delayed until I was twenty-one, but surpassed my own goals.

The only thing that didn't work was my job. I was now manager of the branch and I absolutely hated it. I didn't like going to work as a man, or working in a supermarket, or driving there, or spending every day staring at printouts and fridge freezers and sell-by dates while the checkout girls sneaked into the yard for a cigarette break. I wouldn't have liked it even if the position had been a stepping stone to something better, but it never would be.

This was one of the things I told my new consultant in June. He was a nice man, and I'd be seeing him every three months from now on. I also told him I couldn't see any way of telling Gateway Supermarkets, when the time came, that their manager was now a manageress. I think he took my point; his advice was to change jobs, and he was right, but I didn't have a lot of ideas.

I hated that job so much that I thought I was going to have a breakdown, so I quit and went on holiday to Florida with my brother. We hired a car and had a great time together for three weeks. I told him towards the end of that holiday what I intended to do. He took it as a bit of a joke, as if I was in some sort of extreme phase of gayness and I'd get over it. When it became clear to him that I was serious, he was baffled.

'I can't get my head round this.'

'Well, you're all going to have to get used to it.'

'You're going to tell mum and dad?'

'Of course I am. I have to, don't I? I can't just disappear into one side of the cuckoo clock and reappear with tits and a dress.'

'No. Right. Shit ...well, mate – bloody 'ell. I hope you get out of the house alive.'

When we got back I told my mother. By this time I had long hair, both ears pierced, legs newly waxed and androgynous clothes which I had not worn at home before. I explained about gender reassignment.

'You what?'

I resorted to shorthand. 'I'm getting a sex change.'

'Don't be ridiculous.'

'I am going to be a woman, mum. I'm on a program.'

'Jesus you're out of your tiny mind.'

'That's helpful. Thanks.' I couldn't help it; I started to cry. I'd tried so hard to figure out how to break this to her and it was all going wrong.

'I've always wanted it.'

'No you have not. You've always been perfectly normal.'

'I'm still normal, just not the kind of normal you mean. I've got gender dysphoria, it's a medical condition. It's been diagnosed by two doctors. I've got a consultant's letter...'

'Well he's talking rubbish. You want to get a second opinion.'

'It is a condition and I have it and in order to feel right I need to become a woman. Don't you get it?'

'No. You're wrong. You're wrong. You're listening to the wrong doctors. They put these stupid ideas in your head – I never heard such a load of old rubbish in my life. I'll go to the doctor's with you.'

My father said pretty much the same thing. Yet at some level they must have known for years that something was different about me. I was visibly quite androgynous – at twenty-two I had no facial hair. I thought they'd always been in denial. They certainly were now. There was no acceptance whatsoever. If you respect a person, you take their feelings seriously. I felt they had no respect for me and returned to Liverpool that night feeling hurt and hopeless. I rang them when I got home but nothing had changed. There was ill-feeling and in the months that followed communication between us almost ceased.

I lived in Liverpool from then on and got a job telephone canvassing. I had to ring up people who'd sent off an enquiry form about double glazing asking them to make an appointment. A whole roomful of us worked evening shifts, catching people when they'd just got in after work, talking from a script. We were on a basic salary plus commission. At last I'd found a job that didn't require me to appear in a cheap suit, shirt and tie with a short back and sides haircut.

I was good at it, and was soon managing a team. I was also beginning to live androgynously, and sometimes I'd go clubbing in Manchester after work with my boyfriend. I was happy because I felt I was finally on the right road. My boyfriend wanted to qualify as a nurse and was fine with the idea that I would become biologically female. We saw no problems ahead and thought we had a future together.

Late in the autumn of 1991, almost two years after I had met Dr Hohberger, I was prescribed hormone treatment for the first time.

13 | CHEMICAL WARFARE

The hormone replacement treatment started a chemical war in my body and it devastated me. I felt lost and miserable. I'd expected an initial reaction; maybe a few days of pre-menstrual tension, or post-natal depression, or menopausal mood changes – or one of the things girls talked about. So I knew the hormonal storm was doing this to me and not my rational brain, but it went on and on and I couldn't cope. I couldn't work and had to sign off sick.

Sick pay was paid into the bank. I made the bed, I walked to the shops, I came back and washed up the breakfast things. I plumped cushions, I vacuumed the carpets, I watched the news on TV, I ironed my boyfriend's shirts and hung them up. I started to notice things like smears on glass. I would walk to the corner shop and come back with Windolene and make every window and mirror sparkle. Or I'd decide to clear crumbs from the toaster and spend twenty minutes poking about in it with a bottle brush. Then it would be time to cook supper and I'd start getting a meal together for when my partner came home.

We didn't do much. We watched TV. The television show The Bill often featured criminals from a grotty council estate – I recognised the location as the same place where my dad had been tipped over the balcony.

I had no interest in sex at all. After about a month of this my boyfriend reacted against the whole plan. He wanted the former me back, and thought I should stop taking the tablets.

Our arguments got worse and worse and we ended up spending Christmas of '91 with our respective families. Mine made absolutely no mention of what I had told them in the summer. They had wiped it from their minds. It wasn't as if they didn't want the subject coming up in front of people who didn't know because there was nobody there except me and my siblings. They just didn't want to know themselves.

It was tense and strained and inside I was in turmoil.

I went back to Liverpool and for a while there was a reconciliation. Then my partner decided that I was rejecting sex with him because I was seeing somebody else. I hadn't expected him to have these insecurities but here they were, shouting matches and all, and one February night he threw me out. I'd moved in with him and one night all my stuff was packed and dumped on a wet pavement in Toxteth.

After a week in emergency accommodation I got a train back to London, then Gillingham. Which I hated. I cried a lot. I had to go back to Liverpool to see my doctor and told him how Gillingham felt like ten steps backwards and he gave me a letter for a Housing Department interview. They found me a bedsit in a B&B in Sefton Park, near the city centre. I soon found out that the housing people had told the bedsit owners the situation I was in, which I thought was unnecessary. It certainly didn't help.

I stayed indoors as much as I could and watched the run-up to the '92 General Election on a little television, one of my few possessions. Although I was a Conservative, I was far from the Party's direction of travel. John Major had taken over from Thatcher in 1990 and I still thought she should never have been deposed. The Maastricht Treaty, which was ultimately likely to take us into the eurozone, seemed a bad idea to me, and the Major Government had signed it.

I didn't approach the local Conservative party at all, even to deliver leaflets; I was too distracted by misery and uncertainty. Besides, I knew the Tory win was a foregone conclusion. I thought Kinnock was unelectable and I turned out to be right. As for me, a career in politics was still miles out of reach. I had far more painful and urgent barriers to confront first.

In Liverpool I had no support network other than my doctor. I had always been an outsider to some extent but now I was ill and miserable and I couldn't bear isolation. Soon after the election I was back in Gillingham. Another disaster. There were arguments with my parents about me not having a job, but also about the way I did my hair and dressed. I was wearing androgynous clothes but after months of flooding my endocrine system with female hormones, I was beginning to change shape and look more feminine. I was tall and thin with very little body fat, but by body shape no longer resembled that of a male. My sisters knew what was going on and the older one was harsh about it. The younger one had her own problems as she was unmarried and pregnant.

By June my dad had had enough and told me that if I didn't find somewhere else to live he would hurl my stuff into the street. I'd been there, done that, but at least I knew what to do this time. Gillingham Council had a duty to rehouse me and they did. They found me a tiny bedsit in Chatham; maybe twelve feet by twelve, with a shared kitchen and bathroom.

I decided it was time to make a brave new start. From the day I moved in, on 4 July 1992, I would live entirely as a woman.

My social security payment, after rent was paid, came to £28 a week. Interest rates were soaring, hundreds of thousands of homeowners were in negative equity, and any nine-to-five worker with gumption was competing with the unemployed for a second job. I had no money, I was unwell, and I felt right at the bottom of social ladder. But I couldn't go on like this. I had to get a job.

First I needed a driver's licence, passport and a medical card in my new name Nicole Sinclaire. My quarterly appointments were back at Charing Cross with Dr Hohberger. 'Transsexuals don't have legal rights,' he explained. 'By which I mean you can change your name and all the paperwork, including your passport, to that of a woman as long as you show proof of change of name to the DSS and so on. The only thing you can't change is your birth certificate. Therefore as far as the law is concerned, you were born a man so your gender remains male.'*

* This has changed since.

He told me about a charity, the Gender Dysphoria Trust International (GDTI), that helped people who were going through gender reassignment. They held meetings in somebody's house not far from Chatham and thanks to them I felt less isolated and learned a lot about how to get the paperwork organised. The trust's councilor, Fran Springfield, proved to be invaluable in steering me through those first difficult years.

But when I applied for jobs I was far too diffident. I was a woman concealing my past and of course it showed. I rang up about positions I should have got easily but I heard nothing back. I outlined all the work experience that I'd had, but I always went for low-grade work so that I could start again and the companies wouldn't bother asking for references. I must have seemed evasive and was almost certainly setting off alarm signals.

After all, if someone says they've got junior management level experience in insurance or retail and here they are going for lowly back-office jobs, employers are likely to think they could have been sacked for fiddling the books, or worse. Or that there is some area of their life that they're lying about.

I got no offers at all. The only work I could talk about without reservation or evasiveness was telephone canvassing. The rate of churn is quite high in that industry because it's a stop-gap, second, or holiday job for a lot of people. Often those jobs don't last long – they can be quite specific to particular sales' drives for particular periods. The companies are more interested in your experience and are unlikely to bother with references. If you're no good they know right away because you miss your targets and they get rid of you within a few weeks.

I saw an ad for a job between 6pm and 9pm, six nights a week. 'No Cold Calling', it said, and offered a decent hourly rate plus commission. I phoned up, and the woman on the line seemed interested.

'So can you come in for a chat tomorrow around two o'clock?'

'Yes, fine.'

'And can I take your name – it's Mr -?'

I hesitated for no more than a second; I smoothly gave my old name and put the phone down. I had bottled out. But I thought perhaps I could go there androgynously. And that's what I started to do. I worked there all summer. In my free time I lived as a woman. And slowly I became more confident. One Friday evening the supervisor of the team came over as we were all leaving. She was younger than me and we hadn't talked much.

'You OK?'

'Yes.'

'You're doing well aren't you? I've wanted to ask you for a while. There's something going on with you, isn't there?'

'What d'you mean?'

'I don't know. Look. I'm really embarrassed. So yell at me if you want to because I really don't want to stick my big foot in it.' She hesitated. 'There's something – how do I ...'

'You want to know if I've got issues around my gender.'

'Well I didn't know how to ask. It's none of my business –'

'No, it's fine.'

I wasn't sure that it would be. They could easily get rid of me. But I told her why I was working under my old name, and the changes I'd managed to organise. The result was better than I'd dared to hope. She said I should come in on Monday as a woman. I carried on working as a woman all that winter and it was fine. She even wrote me a letter which I passed to the Gender Identity Clinic at Charing Cross.

The Real Life Test – the Harry Benjamin standard of care – means living your new life, conducting yourself in every social sense in the new way, for a couple of years, and working is part of that. Her letter, and my new bank account showing money going in, my new passport and driver's licence, were proof that I was following the right path.

I was no longer miserable, but still quite passive, reactive rather than proactive; I wasn't setting the agenda of my own life. But I was quietly making progress in the direction I wanted. I was even communicating with my parents again.

Then came my stuck-in-the middle phase.

14 | THE BIG MOMENT ARRIVES

Becoming a woman felt like learning to skate. My friend the supervisor was holding my hand as she guided me round the rink. Then she let go. Her job ended and so did mine and she went to Cyprus for a holiday. I had enough confidence now to keep going alone and got a job as a woman working in telesales for another double glazing company.

When the supervisor came back I was ready to hold her hand again, but I couldn't, because she had sold her house and moved to Cyprus.

I had to make a living so I carried on. I was good on the phone and popular with supervisors. I was also making new heterosexual friends. I was pleased about that. Clothes were easy and I had better dress sense than most of my contemporaries. Mannerisms weren't difficult either as mine had been noticeably feminine. That was the main reason I'd been bullied as a child – kids miss nothing. And even as a man, down the pub after a football match, I'd drawn comment for unconsciously keeping my knees together with my ankles tucked sideways under my chair. I never needed deportment training.

I was living an ordinary life and fitting in. Almost. Although I wasn't gay anymore I was pre-operative. This was complicated. Physically I was still male. I suffered verbal abuse – sarcastic catcalls and wolf whistles, followed by a sneering comment, as I walked down the street. 'Ooh is that a man?' people would whisper. But I think part of the reason was that I was consumed by fear. To say it didn't hurt would be a lie. Of course it does. But when you have imagined doing something so big for so long such slurs become an irrelevance. I knew where I was going and I knew who I was. I might be embarrassed for my friends or family if I was with them at the time but I wasn't going to give the bigots power over my life.

111

Mentally I was adapting to becoming the woman I always felt I was and expected to have a woman's desire for a man. But it wasn't there. My dream was that I'd go through the surgical procedures, find an ideal man, settle down and live happily ever after. I suppose there was a need for affection and human contact because that is an important part of life. Also, when you're in your early twenties, regardless of sexuality, you're encouraged to think that the be-all and end-all of life is to find a partner.

I was on the waiting list for surgery. The snag was funding. This wasn't the kind of waiting list where you move steadily to the top. It was one in which people who get funded first get operated on first. In theory my Local Health Authority would pay the NHS but there was an annual allocation of whatever funds they happened to have. If I'd been unlucky enough to live where there were lots of similar cases it could take years to climb the list.

There wasn't a long queue of candidates for gender reassignment in East Kent (which didn't exactly have a liberal perspective) so the delay for me was probably caused by sensitivity to the public mood. The popular press was screaming about children being refused operations for lack of money while Charing Cross Hospital did 'sex-changes' on the NHS. In the public's mind sex changes were some kind of ooh-er, eye-rolling, yet repellent self-indulgence. Perhaps if there was a better understanding of the syndromes that lead to this momentous decision people would have more respect for those who are forced into it.

Dr Hohburger would ask me how life was going and what difficulties I was facing. He'd ask how I felt about things and whether I'd ever questioned my decision. My future lay in his hands. Before surgery he would have to sign a certificate to say I was mentally competent to undergo the operation. If you're mentally unstable in any way you can't have gender reassignment.

Some doctors prescribe hormones after their very first consultation with patients who appear to have gender dysphoria. This is because the oestrogen and progesterone block testosterone and they'll pretty soon find out whether the person genuinely wants to change sex physically. It's easy for transvestites to self-dramatise: to overstate the significance of their own impulses and mistake their condition for gender dysphoria.

You might think it would make sense (and perhaps it occurred to some doctors in the past) to prescribe extra testosterone to make the issue go away altogether. Extra testosterone is playing with fire. There's always a risk of creating a violent sexual predator. So that is not an option.

A gender reassignment operation is a huge risk. People die – of heart attack, mainly. It's a long and arduous procedure. It isn't simply the cutting-off of testicles that eunuchs used to endure. The penis and testicles have to be removed, the urethra re-directed to an entirely new opening, and a vagina constructed. Secondary surgery usually means breast implantation.

It cost, at that time, about £5,200 to have the one major operation which turns a man's genitalia into a woman's. It was, and I suppose remains, at least seven times more expensive to change a woman into a man because of skin grafts and the even more complex internal physical reorganisation required. The ratio is probably 3:2 male to female. People are surprised by that. This is because woman-to-man transfiguration is often less visible and even less expected. While you may sometimes see a tall woman and wonder, you rarely ask questions about a short man. A tall woman stands out but a short man doesn't. Even then, if he seems somehow womanly people may assume he's a lesbian.

That autumn of '93 my friend came home from Cyprus for a while and I went back with her for a holiday to see whether I liked it. I did and decided to live there. She had bar work in Ayia Napa and I got a job in the cloakroom, thanks to her. (The first Greek phrase I learned was 'Pay me afterwards'. It hasn't worked for Angela Merkel since, but it was useful to me at the time.)

Quite soon I got a job in the club itself. Homosexuality was illegal in Cyprus then – it was a decade before they joined the EU – and Greek Cypriot men being what they were my friend got a lot of flak. Some of them assumed I was her lesbian lover and others thought I was her boyfriend in drag. Our friendship was entirely platonic but these comments made her vulnerable and the friendship became strained.

I moved to Larnaca, and worked in a café. I loved it. I had enough money to keep paying the rent on my little flat in Chatham and save money. I'd been on the waiting list for six months and if I didn't get funded I'd eventually have enough to pay for surgery myself. I flew home every three months to see my family and my doctor and obtain a prescription. Sadly Dr Hohberger died around this time. He had helped so many people.

I was back home during the European Elections of '94 when I became aware of the UK Independence Party (UKIP) that had evolved out of the anti-Maastricht movement. I still called myself a Conservative, but I'd opposed Maastricht at the '92 election so I turned up and helped UKIP deliver leaflets around Gillingham. I also found out more about them. Their national leader was Dr Alan Sked, an academic at the London School of Economics. UKIP was a very liberal Party then and in '97 would advocate legalising cannabis. But I wanted to add my voice to the protest against Gillingham Conservatives, and the Party as a whole, that they were off track on Europe.

All summer the staff at the Gender Identity Clinic kept phoning East Kent health authority to ask about my funding. At last it was granted. My place in the queue was assured and the operation would take place at Charing Cross Hospital early in 1995.

I'd saved quite a lot of money so now I could pay for breast augmentation: £1,980. The hormonal treatment had changed the shape and sensitivity of my breasts already. The surgeon who interviewed me was very careful. He wanted to know what my condition was and why I wanted this done. If I'd walked in off the street he would have refused, but my referral for surgery at Charing Cross satisfied him and I had been living and working as a woman for almost two years.

The operation took place in Hove. I stayed in overnight and had no subsequent problems at all. Mr Porter had done a very good job. I knew, by now, how to wear a bra and how the sizing works. I'd taken a month off work and had a return ticket to Cyprus where I planned to work in the months before the main operation in the New Year.

I was still getting a lot of help from people in the group that Dr Hohberger had recommended. Most of them were moving towards gender reassignment and some were paying for it themselves. They were nearly all over forty. There was one other person as young as me. She had been adopted as a boy, the only child of a well-off couple, and as a man she'd been a teacher. She had wanted to have the operation quickly because she wanted to do nurse training, as a woman, in Eastbourne. The transition phase of hormonal treatment had caused no problems and her parents had paid, so she'd reached the top of the surgical list just nine months after her first interview with a consultant.

You could tell at once that she was an unhappy young woman. People comforted her by saying she was 'adjusting', but the Harry Benjamin principle is to adjust beforehand. She hadn't ever taken the time to do the real life test, and when I met her I recognised its importance. A lot of people say, and they are right, that even after surgery it takes two years to re-adjust your outlook and expectations. I'd dismissed this sort of talk because I'd always known I was a woman, but even for me it turned out to be true. While this woman was at university, studying to be a nurse, she got involved with some Christians who persuaded her to revert and start living as a man again. It was obvious to me that she had made a huge mistake. I thought the whole Christian angle was her excuse to get out of it. Christianity probably offered a psychological escape too. When I last heard she, or he, was in a relationship with a woman.

Older people can adjust better. I still think that if, as a man, this individual had taken the Harry Benjamin pathway he might have either dropped out, or opted for surgery and made the transition to womanhood with a lot less anxiety.

I hope this person found a level of happiness and contentment. The suicide rate of transsexual people is incredibly high. Frustration, fear, rejection and loneliness can be a lethal cocktail.

People say that if you want something badly enough you can get it and that's usually true. If an aim is constantly in view no obstacle or distraction diverts you from your path for long. I'd wanted gender reassignment since long before I knew it was possible to have it and even at my lowest point, in Liverpool, I'd never regretted embarking on this route. That didn't mean I wasn't scared. The younger you start hormone treatment the longer you'll have to take it – which in my case might mean half a century. In the mid-nineties hardly anybody had taken hormone replacement therapy for anything like as long as that. Of those who had been on it for decades, most were biological females who'd reached menopause or had had hysterectomies. Nobody really knew how long I'd need to take HRT. I'd been warned at the outset that its long-term administration might shorten my life by a decade. A decade? I'd been 22. What did ten years lopped off the end matter? In any case, I was sure (and I think I was right) that a fulfilled and happy life for the next fifty years was better than a neurotic unhappy one for sixty.

I was up and about and feeling good when, a few days before I was due back in Larnaca after the breast augmentation, I suffered an unimaginable set back. I'd been bowling merrily along in my car down a country lane near Tunbridge Wells when a lorry braked right in front of me. I slammed my foot on the brake but was about to hit it. Couldn't go left, so I pulled right. Bang. I had a head on collision with a coach.

I was hospitalized in an induced coma for a few days. There was a minor injury to my knee and the steering wheel had put a bad dent in

lulging my passion for football
- Fox Ladies FC 2009

Getting away from it all in Lesbos

the famous Anfield Dressing Room

Supporting AFC Wimbledon's promotion to the
Football League

With the European Cup on the KOP An element of Europe I like!

In more amicable times
with Nigel Farage 2001

As my Nanna used to say,
'There is always someone better than you.'

Campaigning in Medway for the 2001 General Election

With CongressWoman Susan Davis on her
re-election night

With my 'American Moms'

All photos taken from 2002 to 2004
Great friends and a great social life in San Diego

June 2004 With Mike Nattrass on the night of his election to the European Parliament

That Sunday
Telegraph Piece

29th August 2004

On the Campaign trail again during the 2005 General Election in Halesowen

the top of my nose, which looked collapsed and odd. I hadn't been wearing a seat-belt because when you've just had breast augmentation you are told not to. I stayed in the Kent and Sussex Hospital in Tunbridge Wells for a couple of weeks. The accident had one good outcome. My dad hadn't wanted to see me since I'd insisted that the sex change would happen whatever he said about it. My mum had been in touch but dad only really knew what was going on from my brother and sisters. The car crash shook him. He went to see the wreckage of my car and saw at once that if there'd been a passenger in the front seat that person would have died. The whole car had caved in and I had to be cut out of it.

He came to see me when I came out of intensive care. 'Look,' he said, 'I'm not going to argue with you any more. It's your life. You're still my child. I'm glad you're alive.' We were able to rebuild our relationship after that.

My nose would need rebuilding too. I couldn't have corrective surgery to my face, followed by another really major operation, so I decided to keep my place on the list for the main surgery and postpone the cranio-facial procedure until the following year.

When I was discharged I went back to Cyprus and came home a few months later to prepare for the gender reassignment. This meant taking no hormones for eight weeks to reduce the risk of thrombosis. The endocrine system has a huge effect on your emotions and I expected to feel depressed. Knowing what that felt like I dreaded it, and I was right. I struggled to be cheerful. Everything seemed as slow and pointless as it had I'd first started hormone treatment.

It was a difficult time. I was living in Kent with no job. I was waiting to take a risk. The outcome was not entirely certain. It was like standing at the edge of the door of a plane waiting to make a parachute jump; but it went on for week after week.

I'd been told by my consultant psychiatrist, Dr David Dalrymple, who'd taken over Dr Hohberger's patients, that if I had any doubts at all I could consider postponement rather than cancellation. This would at least mean that someone else got my slot in the theatre list. There was only one gender reassignment operation a week, and they did it every Monday. I saw the group less and less, but talked to friends, all of whom knew, and were supportive. I didn't waver.

I went into hospital on Friday night knowing that I'd have to starve all weekend. Your body must be entirely empty. Mine would be a six-hour operation. My surgeon, amazingly, was to be Mr Dalrymple, brother of the psychiatrist.

Dr Dalrymple had already signed me off as in need of treatment. I had a private room, and he visited me on Monday morning to ask whether I was 100% certain that I wanted to go ahead. It is not uncommon for people to lose their nerve only hours before the operation – having of course wasted somebody else's chance of taking the slot. You're vulnerable to fear and not without countervailing pressure. My parents had visited me on the Sunday afternoon. Mum was in tears. 'This is ridiculous. You can just come home.' She was afraid for me. I was about to do a very, very scary thing.

But I had no doubts at all and Dr Dalrymple gave me the consent form to sign. I was wheeled down to theatre and thought 'Good good good', this is right. No anxiety: I was about to become complete. I was given an epidural and thought 'Good, good, good'... The anaesthetist approached, checked the dose, and hovered over me with the needle. 'Good, good, good'...

15 | TELLING LIES

Years later, in another life, I denied that any of this had ever happened.

Why did I lie? It was August, 2004. I'd settled in Southern California, but had been back in England since May working for UKIP before the Euro-elections. The Party had done well, and could now boast a dozen MEPs.

For the sake of my dream job in politics, working for a good friend who'd been elected, I had decided to come back and live in England. I hadn't started work yet, but I'd sold my car and moved into a rented house when, on impulse, I went off for a few weeks to a Greek island with some friends.

Lesbos was a glorious vision of white houses, blue sea, and blue sky. I'd worked hard at the European Elections that year and I lay back and enjoyed it.

Early one evening my phone rang. A journalist identified himself and the paper he worked for.

'Good to talk to you – can I call you Nikki?'

'Yes.'

'You're UKIP's Party Secretary, aren't you?'

'I am, yes.' I would have to step down because of my new job, but that wouldn't start until next month.

'And you wrote to the Pink Paper during the European Elections.'

'I did.' Uh-oh.

'Let me read what you wrote – may I?'

'Sure.' He read it aloud. No problem there. I'd written, in my capacity as Party Secretary, saying that I was gay and that UKIP was not homophobic or it wouldn't have appointed me.

'You stand by that, do you?'

'Of course.'

'Because Christian Voice seem quite hostile.'

'That's their problem.' The Party's image was irredeemable. In this man's mind, the snowy-haired, cardigan-wearing readers of Christian Voice were UKIP voters all. He could well have been right. 'What did you want to know exactly?'

'Do you think it's likely to offend UKIP's membership that you are so open about your sexuality?'

'A few of them, maybe.'

'Most of them, I would have thought. And I hear there's to be a gay splinter group.'

'Not as far as I know.'

'No? So you're not leading it then.'

'No! I've already told the Pink Paper that I was asked to lead a group like that and I refused.'

'Why?'

'Splinter groups are divisive. Obviously.'

'Right. I'm sorry, I need to ask you this. Are you a transsexual?'

'I'm not.'

'You're not.'

'No.'

'Well thank you for your time Ms Sinclair – Oh one more thing. How tall are you exactly?'

'I'm six feet four.'

'Thank you very much. Goodbye.'

The story, when it appeared over three-quarters of a page in the Sunday paper, was headlined 'SIX FOOT FOUR LESBIAN SAYS I WILL NOT BE YOUR LEADER'.

Why did I lie? Nobody in political life should tell a discoverable lie to journalists. You let loose an albatross that hangs around your neck for ever.

Evasion is the standard professional tactic, but my denial was instinctive and from my point of view, not a lie at all. I do not define myself as a transsexual. I used to be transsexual, but I am a woman now.

I'd had a medical condition but it had been corrected, and nobody else has to divulge their medical history so why should I? As it happened, by that time I knew I'd been born with a genetic anomaly, and I had never forgotten the way Caroline Cossey (who'd had exactly the same thing) was treated.

Would it have cost me votes, years later, to reveal it on their terms? Probably. Once you have lied, you cross a line into a fictional world. He asked me how tall I was and I lied about that too. Nearly a decade later, the papers still underestimate my height and journalists still ask (if not warned off beforehand) whether I'm a transsexual. I feel hounded, exasperated. These issues are conventionally put before the public in a way that panders to homophobia and prurience, and that's something I can't change on my own.

There is triage in the NHS these days. Many conditions compete for scarce resources and some lose. Gender reassignment is the condition the public target first. Cosmetic surgery comes a close second. This is sheer ignorance, for psychiatrists will only recommend such procedures to alleviate psychological distress. I can only speak for myself. If I hadn't become a woman I would have led a lonely neurotic life, forever out of place, increasingly depressed and endlessly consulting doctors and therapists at public expense. There are a lot of people like that. As it is I have become a happy, fulfilled achiever and I have repaid, in tax, the cost of my NHS operation many times over.

16 | GETTING THERE

The biggest mistake people make is thinking that once you're a woman following surgery your problem is solved. Well, no. You have changed physically but you still have the same issues – such as being accepted in society. You come to terms with those issues over the following couple of years.

I knew this because I'd had a decade to think about it and discuss it with people who knew. I'd waited till I was sixteen to see a GP, then till I was twenty-one to see a psychiatrist, and at twenty-six, finally ready to go under the knife, I was ready. These ten years had been frustrating and often painful, but I had met and listened to so many experts, and people who'd experienced it, that when it did happen to me, I felt sorted.

I was about to start the life I wanted. I was going to break out of this halfway existence with a body that was in tune with me rather than the other way round. I could go on and do exciting things with my real identity intact.

Eventually.

Early that evening after the surgery I awoke in agony. My back hurt like hell. I pulled the oxygen mask off my face and realised, with mounting fear, that I had no sensation from the waist down. Doctors rushed in. They stuck pins into my thighs and the bottom of my feet. I felt nothing.

I was given morphine for a screaming pain in my back. My parents were there but I couldn't speak. Nor could I sleep properly, because nurses came in every twenty minutes to observe my blood pressure, temperature and other vital signs.

On Tuesday morning I had some feeling in my toes. I fell asleep and woke up that afternoon. I could feel my legs now and the pain in my back was less excruciating.

I wasn't allowed to eat until the following Saturday. I could have Bovril, and I had to drink a specific amount of water daily since my bladder had been moved to a new position and this would help prevent infection. I could not eat since a full bowel puts pressure on the bladder. And I was packed up with padding inside because my body's natural reaction would be to revert – to 'make itself right' – by pushing all my internal organs back to where they'd been before.

All the surgical packing was to be removed five days later. With every day that passed I felt better. I read, watched television, and listened to music.

I couldn't even get out of bed, as I was catheterised. There was a horrible smell. I couldn't have a bath, I'd lost a lot of blood, and all my waterworks were re-arranged. I felt disgusting.

'Don't worry, not long till Saturday,' the nurses said reassuringly. Great. I felt disgustingly dirty. The stench of dried blood and perspiration was revolting.

On Saturday morning when the packing had been taken out I was helped out of bed and taken to the toilet. It was the weirdest sensation. If you've changed your gender you know nothing about muscle control. You are using muscles differently, and it's messy at first. The nurse explained how to use the right muscles, but I'd have to practise.

Then, the greatest thing in the world: I had a hot, medicated ,bath, and clean linen on the bed. This was bliss. I would have to have salt baths for months to come. And I had to learn to dilate, because your body has an inbuilt urge to close an opening. If you're born a woman you'd think it's easily done, but it isn't. The first couple of times it's quite frightening.

I would stay in hospital for a few more days. I couldn't safely walk very far and I began to have pains in my calf muscles. Doctors reassured me that it was probably just cramp. This was an error on their part. DVT (deep vein thrombosis) is one of the major post-operative dangers of surgery like mine, because of the turmoil your entire system is in and the fact that you must remain immobile for a long time. They knew this, and I was given anti-coagulant treatment, but it was not enough. I was discharged in pain. I could not stand up straight or walk upright. I thought this must be because I'd been in bed for a week – but there was rather more going on.

I was told to keep moving around and I'd be fine. I went home but the pain was getting worse and worse . My dad drove me to the doctors.

'It's cramp,' he said. 'You've just had a major operation, you have to keep moving.'

Dad drove me home. I limped very slowly into the house, and collapsed in agony in the living room with blinding pain behind my knee. Mum called an ambulance. Pains in my abdomen began as the ambulance arrived.

I was taken to A&E at the Medway Hospital where a doctor spotted DVT immediately and shot me full of anti-coagulants. The clot had been travelling up my body and his swift action saved my life.

DVT is promoted by immobility, but bizarrely, I now had to spend another week in bed, in hospital. I was supposed to be getting regular salt baths and learning to dilate but the hospital really didn't want to know; they hooked me up to a heparin drip so I couldn't get about. In my second week the drip was removed, but walking was still agony, because although the clot had dispersed it had done some damage. I'd now spent a month mostly in bed, my muscles were wasted, and I was fearful of falling and hurting myself internally.

I was terrified. I had come very close to dying after achieving everything I had always wanted. That summer was another difficult one. I was taking Warfarin and at one stage was taking 21 hormones, anti-coagulants, painkillers and anti-inflammatories every day. How on earth were they all going to interact? Nobody seemed to know. Separating the areas of medical expertise into psychiatric pain and physical pain seems inappropriate in those circumstances. Mind and body are interlinked. Everything affects everything else.

I had to visit the hospital twice a week. I could not walk far and I was living on benefits in a flat in Gillingham with too few friends. Because I had become a semi-invalid I wouldn't be suitable for cranio-facial surgery as soon as I'd hoped. I didn't adjust well to this. Except for my nightmare months of hormone storm, I'd been an active and energetic person. This was different. It was easy to slide into resignation about being incapacitated. My life seemed to lurch without event from one hospital appointment to the next. I was told to get out and walk. Walk where? What for? All I wanted to do was hide myself, to be safe in my little room. So I didn't make much progress, because the less I walked about, the more painful walking remained.

I once saw a mynah bird in a cage. The door was open, but it wouldn't come out. It had become habituated to the safety of entrapment. I knew of other people who'd ended up quietly isolated for good after surgery. When you can't see progress, you get discouraged and give up, settling for a passive life alone; sans risk, sans joy, sans travel, keeping pain at bay. You can get agoraphobia. I wasn't frightened to go out, exactly, but I definitely preferred not to. I would get the family to bring essentials – things like milk and bread – when they visited, and once the cupboard was stocked, I'd be relieved. I behaved as though I was besieged by the world outside.

I watched TV and re-read my books. Robert Kilroy Silk's programme, Kilroy, was on every morning. (Kilroy Silk had been an academic and a Labour MP who fell out with Neil Kinnock over the party's failure to control its more Militant elements.) His programmes were issue-based, and one was all about transsexuals. The man himself, famous for his good looks and, it was said, his tendency to preen, was a political maverick, with an enthusiastic following among housewives.

He was a politician at the height of his persuasive power. If I learned anything from him I did so sub-consciously. The whole idea of becoming a politician, which had been at the back of my mind for as long as I could remember, seemed as remote as it had been before the operation. In those days I'd been physically fit, but psychologically I couldn't have done it. Now I wasn't physically fit, I had lost nearly thirty pounds, and was fast becoming melancholic as well. I'd morphed into one of the incapacitated thousands who are on benefit for years.

My mental state needed managing and I was taking too many conflicting treatments at once. I should have been seeing a post-operative counselor, instructed by Charing Cross. But that person didn't exist. My GP offered anti-depressants. I went to the chemist's with my prescription. The tablets were in a blue and white box. I kept it in the kitchen. If I took even one of those things I would be admitting that I had lost control of my life. I never opened the packet. It stayed there for ages. That blue and white box was my constant reminder of the wrong way to go.

In 1996 I was able to walk further and finally roused myself to action. In the spring I ventured forth on buses and trains. I joined UKIP and later that year became the local branch Secretary. I started going into London. At matinees, if you can prove you're on benefits, you get big discounts. Everything changed. I was beginning, at last, to move forward; I felt positive again.

17 | NEW ME, NEW POLITICS

In the summer of '96 I was well enough to think about what I was going to do. My nervousness and depression had been lifted by action and mental stimulation. I decided to go back into education in September and contacted the local college. I was interested in law, but I'd left Woolwich before finishing my A-levels so I got into a one-year, full-time Access course.

A lot of mature women were going back into education then and the Access course followed conventional school terms and school hours so that they could be at home for their children. But in term times, they needed about thirty free hours every week for lectures, research and coursework and many of my class dropped out. They began with high hopes, but if you lack confidence, have an unsupportive partner, demanding dependents or a difficult journey – or all of the above plus money worries – you have to be spectacularly focused to clear all that time for study.

Fortunately I was single and would be able to live on my resources with no problems. I was still taking a lot of hormones and was far from fully mobile. Charing Cross had issued guidance, but it wasn't specific enough for my circumstances. I'd reacted badly to the first operation, but I was still taking hormones and I'd be having further surgery in the middle of my first term, in October, at Charing Cross again. I'd been made to stop taking these hormones before, so this time I made it clear that I wanted expert advice.

I had an appointment with a senior endocrinologist. Since Charing Cross was a teaching hospital and mine was an unusual case, the consultation was, with my permission, in the presence of a lot of students. He wanted to know the whole story, starting with when I'd first known I had to be a girl.

129

One of the things he suggested, which someone else had brought up earlier, was that I might have some type of chromosomal condition. I wasn't bothered, really. I felt physically OK; I just wanted reassurance or a lower dose of hormones if necessary. He asked me if I'd have some tests – lots of them, not just blood tests.

The blood tests showed that I lacked testosterone. Too much oestrogen and progesterone had knocked it out, and apparently – and this was new to me – women need testosterone too, to strengthen their bones among other things. My doses of Premarin, extracted from the urine of pregnant mare's, was drastically reduced.

These results left me largely unmoved, although the endocrinologist and his students were immensely excited. Apparently I had been born with Klinefelter Syndrome, in which the chromosomal pattern is XXY, (the male norm is XY). But my chromosomal pattern is XXXY. In other words I have two extra X-chromosomes. (Before I began to think of myself as a creature from outer space, the endocrinologist reassured me that although this is pretty rare, people can have even more – both Xs and Ys.)

I've read about Klinefelter since. Like Harry Benjamin, he was a doctor. He was the first to identify and classify the syndrome. There's a wide variety of effects among men who have it and I had some fairly typical symptoms, including, besides gender dysphoria, the dramatic height gain, the difficulties at school and the small but long hands and feet. (My brother, who is an inch and a half shorter than me, wears size fourteen shoes while I wear ten-and-a-half.) Physical symptoms tend to appear at puberty and gender dysphoria can be absent altogether in men whose pattern is the commoner XXY.

Frankly I'd now lived through the whole issue and put it behind me. The last thing I wanted to do was revisit it. But I'd had a lot of tests I'd never had before and once the endocrinologist identified my condition, he wanted to do even more.

I, however, wanted to look forward. Things were beginning to happen in my life. I was no longer a person with a gender issue. I didn't want to be pulled back into this.

'So,' I asked him: 'How significant is this likely to be for me?'

'Oh... Not very. If you were a man you might have a higher than usual chance of being infertile, but that's...'

'Exactly,' I said. 'That's not my concern any more is it?'

So he had to give up on me. His loss of an experimental subject was my gain. I was starting a new life. And I'd only have to take one HRT tablet a day.

My Access to Law course had begun and I was happy. I developed a grasp of critical thinking, legal reasoning, researching and essay-writing and made friends. We'd sit together talking and arguing about John Stuart Mill, a 19th Century MP and political philosopher; I wrote reams in the margins of my Penguin copy of his book 'On Liberty'. This was everything I'd hoped for. When I had to take my weeks off for facial surgery in the first term, the tutors helpfully provided lecture notes and photocopies. The corrective operation went well, except for that moment when I looked in the mirror too soon, saw my huge swollen head, and yelped. It had deflated, fortunately, by the time I went back to college.

In the spring term of 1997 the college organised a coach trip to the European institutions in Strasbourg, Brussels and Luxembourg for students from our course. The debate about the EU single-currency and EU membership was hotting up before the General Election in May. Jimmy Goldsmith's Referendum Party was gaining traction and the Conservative Party was still torn apart over Maastricht.

Current affairs were a focus for debate and learning to argue one's case was an important part of the syllabus. Once, we had a debate about the single currency and I was chosen to lead the argument in favour. I didn't mind, because the best way to win any argument is to understand the other side's point of view. As it happened I won that debate. It didn't change my opinions, and I carried on with UKIP. I invited a group of friends from the course to a UKIP meeting. Our local candidate wasn't much older than me, but it was all too noticeable that most of the members were retired. For a political party, ours was a disastrous demographic; too little appeal to the majority, and your constituency dies off. Also, many old people are not able to take an active role. Activists are the engine of a political party.

I enjoyed the coach trip so I was most indignant when I was thrown off at Strasbourg, our first stopover.

After we'd been shown around the main chamber of the Parliament we were taken to one of the meeting rooms for a debate with a Labour MEP, Peter Skinner. I went for the jugular, with all my new debating skills.

'What are you doing here?' I asked him.

'I'm representing the people of West Kent.'

'How can you claim to represent them?' I countered.

'They are EU citizens, so they're entitled to representation in this Parliament.'

'I was made a citizen of the EU, we all were, but I didn't ask to be. None of us gave the politicians the permission to do that.'

'Yes, you became a citizen by indirect representation, but I would argue that you gain from it. You gain influence because we represent you.'

'I want to know how you can claim to represent us at all. The politicians we elect to the British Parliament have less power, because we're in the EU, than they would have if we didn't belong to it. So why would we ever think it's a good idea to let the EU rule over us?'

'But that's how it is. Successive Governments have delegated powers to the wider forum of the EU. And the electorate gave consent when they elected Governments.'

'But who said you could do this?'

'Again, I have to say, the people of West Kent ...'

And so it went on with me making the point that we elect politicians to Westminster but that we have never had a referendum on whether or not to become EU citizens and devolve real power to Brussels.

Peter Skinner had had a good argument, and maybe I was too assertive – but I was taking the first chance I'd ever had to put my point of view to someone in a perceived powerful position.

I was told I'd embarrassed the college and they sent me home. I didn't get to go to Luxembourg or Brussels. I could choose to stay on the coach if I wanted, but I wouldn't be allowed into any of the institutions. Another woman, a friend called Pam, had a dispute about something else and also left with me.

Did the lecturers over-react? I think so. Maybe they didn't want to give the impression that they'd taught me all this stuff; or maybe they were worried about consequences for the EU-funded European Library at the University of Kent in Canterbury. The College was part of the University of Kent. Also they probably didn't want me let loose on the unelected bureaucrats at the Commission in Brussels, our next stop, which was where the real power resided.

I was quite well informed on the EU at the time. I ignored everything I was taught, which was almost without exception in favour of it. Eurosceptics were a minority in the class, and in the population; apathy was a more characteristic reaction.

Most people didn't bother forming an opinion. It was all too difficult and distant. All the same, I plunged enthusiastically into work for UKIP as it prepared for the General Election. When I tried leaf-letting, the pains in my legs returned, which was frustrating, but I was still in recovery from the deep vein thrombosis damage. I had to do something useful, preferably from behind a desk. Then Craig McKinley, the Deputy Leader asked if I would do some data entry at UKIP's HQ in Regent Street.

At last! Just when I least expected it, and after years of trying, I finally had a job in London – with my travel paid for and a decent hourly rate. I could juggle the coursework, help UKIP in Gillingham, and this new job would take me into London just after the morning rush hour, two days a week. I would be busy, which is what I love most.

Of course at the elections, late in May, Tony Blair celebrated a landslide victory. 'ThIIINgs can only get BETTER!'. Cool Britannia. All that. Then it was very bliss to be alive – for New Labour.

Looking back, the outcome seems inevitable. The electorate voted about education, the NHS, sleaze, and the arrogance of Conservatives in power. Above all, people wanted a change and they were not much interested in the Euro, so the only significant result of UKIP and Jimmy Goldsmith's Referendum Party at that time was to reduce Conservative votes.

New Labour were very pro-EU. Giving independence to the Bank of England was a requirement preceding membership of the single currency and it was the first thing Gordon Brown did once he'd parked his toothbrush in Number 11. Soon afterwards he had to go to Brussels to get permission from the Commission to reduce VAT on domestic fuel. The rate introduced by Major's government had been 8%, which was handing Labour an open goal. They'd leapt up thundering that this was an attack an on the vulnerable, which it was. What the Tories wouldn't admit was that they'd had to do it because of laws passed in Brussels. Ken Clarke had been Chancellor at the time and later he tried to put it up to 15%.

Brown negotiated a reduction to 5%, where it is now, and tried to counter its ill effects with a fuel allowance for the elderly. Given that not all old people were poor, and too many children and disabled people were living in poverty, this was an inadequate response. I felt, and still do, that VAT should be removed from domestic fuel altogether. But our new government had to kow-tow to Brussels. In practice, Labour do not represent the vulnerable

In June 97 I passed my Access to Law course, so next term I'd be a first-year law student at the University of Kent in Canterbury. I went on working at UKIP then got a job managing a telephone canvassing team. I'd set it up from scratch with someone else from the course and most of the people we employed were from our class. We earned decent money all that summer.

In October, when we began our first term on the LLB degree course, this small workforce disbanded and I spent my time in Canterbury at the University. I was still working for UKIP in Regent Street a couple of days a month, but around this time they took a nosedive. There was a leadership crisis and Alan Sked left. The man I helped, Craig McKinley, became interim leader before an election, when the membership chose Michael Holmes. Neither of them made a huge impression on the British public.

When Jimmy Goldsmith died we got the Referendum Party lists too. It was a good match. UKIP in those days emphasised its leaders' life experience outside politics. This contrasted with the public's view, in the last days of the Tory Government, that politicians were even less trustworthy than estate agents.

UKIP's leadership brought experience in business, or occasionally in education or medicine – but it also brought the prejudices of the cricket club and had little appeal to younger women, the poor, or northerners. And there were no women at the top of the Party.

Meanwhile I was continuing to adapt to my new life as a woman. There were unexpected challenges for me ahead. Sex with men, as a woman, was okay. It was a bit weird losing your virginity for a second time, but if I'd had to rate the thrill, I'd have given it three out of ten. I told myself that sex hadn't done much for me at school the first time, but still, it worried me. I was a woman now. I enjoyed the company of men. There were things I wanted from men. I thought maybe I should just relax about this. I was not in need of a partner, after all – I had lots of things to do, to achieve. In April '98 I did once notice myself looking with interest at a woman, and wondered about my feelings, but I put the thought aside.

Everything was going really well. The day after my first year exam at the end of May, I was at Heathrow with a full backpack and an Air New Zealand round-the-world ticket, knowing that I didn't need to return until October. I spent a night in a hotel in Bangkok and flew to Australia. When you are travelling, you have time to think. I went into some women's bars in Oxford Street, Sydney, and felt okay. I didn't feel out of place, but nor did I identify with the people there.

There were thousands of miles of Australia and I had the time to explore them, so I bought an Oz tour ticket, a bit like a Eurorail pass but for minibuses. These tours were brilliant; I met lots of new people from all over the world, friendships that still endure today. I felt included and accepted.

The first big stop was Canberra, the Capital and seat of government, in the ACT (Australian Capital Territory) or as the straight-talking Aussies refer to it 'Arseholes Congregating Together.' I stayed a few days, visited the old Parliament and the new one, which wasn't in session. Instead I ducked inside the Aboriginal tent embassy opposite the old Parliament. It's been there since the 1970s and looks like a shack in Soweto. It's a hangout, a drop-in centre. The people inside explained their adamant rejection of the two-hundred-year-old European claim to Terra Australis. They said this was their land, not the white man's property, and they wanted some recompense, because in their view every non-Aborigine who went to Australia was there illegally. You could choose to negotiate if both parties agreed and they offered me the opportunity to do so. So I did and they gave me a document that said I had permission to be in Australia.

I continued to travel on the Oz tour bus. This was my own stab at a gap year, ten years late. I went to an Aussie Rules football match at the Melbourne Cricket Club and visited the set of Neighbours.

Christchurch, New Zealand, came next. And it was here that I realised that I was definitely looking at women, though I didn't do anything about it. In fact I went around the world with that question about how I felt about women at the back of my mind. I just didn't put a label on it. I had not made a decision through a process either – there seemed no need to do so.

In Christchurch I ended up in a lesbian-run women-only hostel: a NO MEN ALLOWED within fifty yards of the gate sort of place. Otherwise it was like a hotel, but at backpackers' rates. A much older woman ran it for the benefit of younger women. It was fine; no romantic interludes, but I didn't feel threatened either. Everyone seemed friendly.

I spent my 30th birthday in Kaikoura, on New Zealand's South Island, swimming among a huge shoal of wild dolphins. It was transformative. You interpret their sweet nature as you wish, and for me, I felt validated and valued. (You cannot experience this in a tank in Florida.)

I crossed the Cook Strait to Wellington and managed to observe the New Zealand Parliament in action. There was a woman Prime Minister, Jenny Shipley, and Labour Opposition Leader Helen Clarke. It was the most ferocious Question Time I had ever seen in my life – similar to the British system but with the gloves off – vicious, attacking stuff with none of the circumlocution and false politeness that lowers the temperature in the House of Commons.

The rest was just fun; snorkelling, bungee jumping, parties in Fiji and California until September

The day after I got back to the UK in September, I was back at work for UKIP in the West End of London. They'd achieved a 13.2% swing in a first-past-the post by-election result in Yorkshire. But the Euro elections were to be decided by proportional representation, so if that result had been replicated countrywide, they'd have nine or ten more MEPs. Things were looking up.

I was still attracted to men, especially those who were about a decade older than me, as I had been when I was a gay male. I like spending time with people who have interesting things to say regardless of who they are. Yet I was definitely having feelings about women as well. By this time I'd had enough anxiety around gender for ten lifetimes, so I gave up worrying about it and started going to a bisexual group in the Caledonian Road, in London on Friday nights and onto clubs afterwards with some of them.

In October, at half term, I went with one of the bisexual group members to Ibiza and then on to Cyprus. I hadn't been there for four years, and I ended up having sex with a man. This time I was certain. I thought 'I don't like this. I don't want to do this anymore.'

I had met a woman in Liverpool and had my first lesbian experience – uncharacteristically, a one-night stand . This was much, much better than sleeping with a man, but it also registered as a step along what I feared could be a difficult path.

Was this the kind of woman I was meant to be? I began to have misgivings. I really did not want to be a lesbian. I had enough difficulties without being gay again. Maybe that night in Liverpool had been an aberration, I thought. I had also begun seeing a man I liked.

18 | A NIGHT TO FORGET

It was Monday, 26 April, 1999 and my thoughts, since lunchtime, had been on the news that Jill Dando – the presenter of television programme 'Crimewatch' – had been found shot dead on the front path of her house in Fulham. The murder seemed random and was therefore doubly shocking. Or was it a stalker? People had talked about it at the bar that evening, and speculated about what had happened.

These thoughts were swirling through my head as I drove home to Gillingham, in Kent, after attending the bisexual women's group at the Drill Hall in Bloomsbury, London.

I was living in Gillingham and had built my coursework around UKIP – where I had been selected as a candidate for the North West Region – the bisexual group of women, and dates with the man. I travelled to Liverpool on the weekends and listened to any lectures I'd missed at my course on tapes from the library, in my car, during the drive from Liverpool back down to London.

But on this drive from Bloomsbury to Kent, I suddenly regretted not having used the loo before leaving the women's meeting. I needed to go, and there was an hour's journey ahead of me to Gillingham.

Scanning the road for a public toilet I spotted one of those modern coin-operated cubicles on the Commercial Road, just after the turn-off to the Isle of Dogs. It was on a long spit of concrete between the main highway and a parallel slip road, where I could pull over and park. Desperate by now for the loo, I hurried across to the booth.

It was close to midnight and there were very few pedestrians along this busy road; just the relentless roar of traffic as fast-moving headlights streamed by in both directions. I came out of the cubicle, crossed the slip-road and was rummaging in my bag for the car keys when my arm was gripped and my leg kicked.

I gasped, overbalanced and landed painfully with a suffocating weight on top of me and a big greasy hand slapped tight across my mouth. He stank of stale body odour. I saw that he was tall and heavy set, and got a flash of white face, the side of it, before I shut my eyes. He was screaming in a London accent: 'I'll fucking kill you! Fuck you! Fuck you!' as he ripped my pants down and raped me. I remember he had terrible breath which reeked of stale tobacco.

The attack seemed to go on and on – I kept my eyes squeezed tightly shut throughout. I didn't dare have him think I'd seen his face or that I could identify him. I didn't dare anything. I kept thinking: 'has he got a knife?' I kept thinking a lot of things. Finally he got off me and bolted. My eyes stayed shut as I listened to his feet pounding away until I knew he was gone.

I lay immobile, on the cold, dirty pavement, for a long time. Nobody walked past me. I tried to take deep breaths, to clear my mind, to stop thinking about anything. Finally I opened my eyes. Some of the street lamps went out. I noticed and thought they must be on a timer. My car was parked between me and the endless traffic. I felt totally worthless and humiliated.

Eventually I got up, pulled my clothes back together and got back to my car. A newspaper with the headline about Jill Dando was lying on the passenger seat beside me.

I drove shakily home and sat on my bed. I desperately wanted a bath. I knew I shouldn't wash so that samples could be taken, but I had a lot of reasons for not going to the police. I didn't know what to do. The man who attacked me was a dangerous rapist. And he was still out there.

I phoned a friend from the course, who was a nurse. She came round and we talked about it.

'You've got to report it,' she insisted. 'I'll come with you.'

'No. Even if they catch him they won't charge him. They can't! You know that.'

Under the law that prevailed at that time, I existed as a man, and vaginal rape was therefore impossible. There had been test cases.

'No, it'll be a serious sexual assault. But even so –'

'And look at the way the police are.'

I didn't have to explain. They were notoriously unsympathetic to rape victims. It was common knowledge that even if they didn't disbelieve you outright, they'd imply that you'd 'asked for it' or somehow diminish your rape to an assault. Today, still, women are often treated unfairly even years after they've been the victim of rape, with the attack being used as a warped sort of ammunition against them.

'If you go with DNA evidence,' she said patiently, 'they've got to take action.'

'Then what?'

'If he's on a database fine, and if he's not, they keep it because he'll probably do it to somebody else before he's caught. That's why we need to go to the police.'

'No, I've really thought about this. Can you imagine what it'd be like in court?'

'It'll be embarrassing, but...'

'I won't be believed by a jury.'

'You'll have evidence.'

'Evidence. How can I produce evidence of rape if it isn't technically rape? I know I'm not making sense but it's not about that. He'd claim consent – it's not impossible, I've been seeing a man. And imagine what his barrister would say.' I put on a voice. "So he overcame you. I see. And how tall are you, exactly, Ms Sinclaire?' He'd get off.'

I was negative about this partly because in the back of my mind was my dad's experience from all those years ago. Then, as now, there had been no witnesses. My attacker had been a six-footer, but as with dad in Carshalton, if you catch someone bigger unawares, you can use shock and leverage to overwhelm them. That man had been a lot heavier than me – I was thin for my height – so it hadn't been that difficult. Then came the fear. I'd frozen.

How could I ever explain this to a hostile court with the man standing there? Would the mere fact of gender change prejudice a jury against me? I was under no illusions. His defence would certainly make the most of it. And even if he didn't get off, he'd be out, sooner or later. I remembered living with dad's attacker in Carshalton. You never felt safe.

We compromised. At 9am my friend took me to a clinic in Dartford where they took swabs and kept them so that if I changed my mind they would be available. They also photographed the bruises. My whole body was brown, yellow and purple – especially my thighs and upper arms. In the aftermath of the ordeal, I found it difficult to articulate my emotions. I didn't cry once.

Friends were supportive and so were the people at UKIP. I told Heather, who ran Head Office, what had happened and she'd sent flowers. And Fabian, who worked long hours at Head Office as a volunteer and was in his seventies, was really sweet when I eventually saw him again. My brother was furious. My mother knew, but I don't think my dad did. For a long time I couldn't stop thinking about it. In a flash of annoyance I phoned the police one night and told a policewoman what had happened. I was asked my name but I wouldn't give it.

'How can we help if we don't know your name?' she said.

I put the phone down.

I went backwards. I had another HIV test after the attack. It was negative. But I didn't take my second year exams. I withdrew as a candidate. The University provided a counsellor. The whole month of May was a complete washout. I went back to sitting alone in my flat. The news was full of Jill Dando for a long time.

I stopped going out; no UKIP, no university and no groups, however supportive. Saddest of all was that the attack had put a dent in my lifelong love affair with London – my favourite city in the world where I had always felt accepted, and more importantly safe.

With rape, reporting rates are low. Conviction rates are low too; I would probably have hurt myself more than the rapist if I'd reported it.

The rape was terrible, but my reaction to it – vulnerability, a sense of being lost, a ridiculous sense of guilt – was apparently normal. But it didn't unbalance me for long. After four weeks I kicked myself into action. I would do something from my bucket list. I went to Chatham High Street, where there were still travel agents, and bought the first flight available – which happened to be one to Salzburg from Gatwick. I hired a car. I drove until I found somewhere to stay on my first night in Austria. Then I settled down to watch Manchester United win the European Cup. This was of course torture, given my deep loathing of Man United as a Liverpool supporter. I could have stayed home and got furious there. But little steps...

The next ten days I spent driving around Central Europe, employing all the map-reading skills I'd learned at school. I had no plans. I stopped wherever I saw interesting things. I would drive all day, find a hotel in the early evening, and leave early in the morning, travelling in a zig-zag circle, barely stopping, from Salzburg through Munich into the Czech Republic, through Pilsen, Prague, Brno, to Katowice in Poland and Krakow; and into Slovakia where I stopped in Bratislava before driving to Vienna and back to Salzburg.

I came back well enough to attend the UKIP pre-election rally at the Chatham Dockyard in the first week of June. Afterwards Nigel Farage came up to me and asked if I was all right. He was very sympathetic, angry on my behalf, and asked was there anything he could do. He seemed perfectly sincere and I was very pleasantly surprised. He seemed so kind. I'd known him since 1997, but I hadn't necessarily thought of him as that sort of person. He'd seemed like a bit of a joke, in his pinstripe suit that reminded me of Arthur Daley.

A few days later Nigel got elected as an MEP. He'd always been influential in the Party, because he charmed old ladies. Success in the polls was a terrific distraction for me; it demonstrated that we were a professional Party and could win our argument. We had three MEPs in Europe for the next five years – all from the south and east of England. In the nineties UKIP benefited from disillusioned ex-Tory voters, although since then they have cut a swathe through the old Labour constituencies in the Midlands and North.

19 | A POLITICAL EDUCATION

I'd deferred my third year at university, so I was working full-time at UKIP Head Office that summer when some new jobs became available. I was shortlisted to be Nigel Farage's assistant and one of the questions at the interview was: 'You know he can be quite a difficult person to get on with. How would you deal with that?' I told them that I'd insist on having an inflatable Nigel Farage doll to keep in a cupboard, so that when he frustrated me I could punch it. They all burst out laughing.

It's probably just as well somebody else got that job, but I was recommended to take up another London post when the current incumbent left.

I had also begun my first relationship with a woman. Though it lasted only a few months it led me to realise that I not only preferred sex with women but that I reached a level of contentment in their company that I had never achieved with men. I still think very fondly of her.

An internal war broke out within UKIP that autumn. Michael Holmes, who was still Leader, distrusted the National Executive and fell out with them. From then on there were effectively two warring parties; UKIP in London and UKIP/Holmes in Salisbury. Nigel Farage, playing Prince Rupert behind the scenes, oversaw a raid on our HQ in Regent Street. The UKIP database was removed along with all our files and computers. Fortunately, I had had the foresight to make a copy, both digitally and paper documents. This enabled us to re-establish the Head Office in Regent Street.

At the time, nobody blamed Nigel, who had managed to plant a foot in each camp.

We couldn't continue as a divided Party, so in the New Year this skirmish was followed by a pow-wow: an Extraordinary General Meeting at Central Hall, Westminster. UKIP had about eight thousand members at the time and about a thousand of them were in the hall. By the end of the morning the leaders from both sides had been booted out and a decision made to re-form the fifteen-man (yes, they were all men) National Executive.

I stood for election to the new executive. There were seventy-two candidates and I came twenty-third. I think I was the youngest candidate. Afterwards I recognised that I'd saved myself a lot of trouble by failing to get elected. One woman did get in, but she was immediately disqualified for having used a photograph of herself that was twenty years out of date (despite a UKIP officer allowing the picture to be used). It was a frankly sexist outcome in a sexist set-up. The NEC always held their meetings in gentlemen's clubs where women were admitted, on sufferance, to certain areas other than the bar.

I then stood as UKIP candidate for Medway Council. Between March and May 4, 2000, the day of the local elections, I went knocking on doors, talking to voters and leafleting. That was proper campaigning. I had to test myself, although I was worried about getting snide coverage in the local press. Gender reassignment was still made out to be shameful. 'Perverts,' my dad had said, all those years ago. They say words can't hurt you, but they stay in your mind. I kept telling myself that if the press queried my gender because somebody I'd known in my former life said something, any scandal would be of purely local interest.

Nobody said a word. When the results came out and I got 13.2% of the vote, I was pleased. One of the sub-headlines on an article in the local paper was 'Too tall an order' – but that was all. It was quite a good experience.

In May I re-took my second year exams and passed, and carried on with my job at UKIP. I was now Head Office manager and able to rent a two-bedroom flat in Docklands with a friend. In October I'd be starting my final year at university.

Yet again, I failed to focus on one thing at a time. That summer the rented apartment became a millstone. The second bedroom turned out to be damp, the rent was high and the landlord wouldn't get the problem fixed. The friend got fed up with it, so I found someone else to share, but that person moved to somewhere cosier as well, and the landlord still refused to get anything done about the damp. Given that I was getting only half the value, I started paying only half the rent. Maybe I hadn't revised the law on rental property or maybe I was just being spectacularly dumb, but this was not a good move.

October came, and I tried to do my full-time third-year course part-time because I didn't want to lose my job. The flat was a worry, and by Christmas I was struggling with the course. I was stumbling on both fronts. What do I do when I'm worried? Take radical action in a different direction. So I became UKIP's candidate for Medway in the General Election which was planned for May 2001.

I was now much more well known in the Party, and a parliamentary candidate, so I decided to stand for election to the National Executive Committee for a second time; and this time I was sure I'd get in. Unfortunately the existing members of the NEC didn't want me and in defiance of the Party's constitution, rushed through a rule that no employee could be on the NEC. So although I was elected, I was immediately disqualified.

I made a hoo-ha and subsequently lost my job. I now had no job, no NEC seat, an unscrupulous landlord hounding me for money, final exams in less than five months, and two budding legal disputes with UKIP over unfair dismissal and unconstitutional action. But I was standing for Parliament in June so that's where I concentrated my resources.

I was learning a lot. But I was neither dealing with the troublesome landlord nor revising for my law degree. I tried to defer my finals, but it wasn't possible. So I stopped being a student. At the same time I got notice to quit my flat and stopped paying rent, retreating to my own tiny flat in Gillingham.

The General Election was due in May but the dreadful Foot and Mouth epidemic, with its officially sanctioned mass slaughter of cattle, dragged on. Since traffic around the country was discouraged, there seemed every reason to keep polling stations shut and the election was postponed until June. Though rank outsiders, we did well in Medway, though we lost our deposit.

The Docklands landlord, or rather his lawyers, ratcheted up the pressure. Both sides were too stubborn and legal fees were escalating.

I had a lawsuit coming my way from him. I was taking UKIP to an employment tribunal. I was also taking them to the High Court over their sneaky rule change. Money was tight. I had to take drastic action.

I also decided I needed more political experience and wanted to return to America for the experience of an election campaign. So I wrote to the Republicans and the Democrats in nearly every state (avoiding the ones I really didn't want to live in, like Utah) saying that I could fund myself – though expenses would be appreciated – and that I would love to help with an election campaign.

I posted about ninety applications and waited.

In the meantime I prepared for an Employment Tribunal hearing in Tavistock Square. (UKIP's lawyers erroneously claimed that I had failed in the proper execution of my duties, and made an accusation about petty cash – which I refuted by showing I had put myself out of pocket. I got about £4,500 in compensation.)

I wasn't so lucky with the landlord. The court found in his favour and ordered me to pay his costs – an eye-watering £22,000. I would never forget the state of that flat, and was determined he wasn't getting my money. Besides, I had a ticket to San Diego to buy, and accommodation to find, after receiving a letter from the Democrats in California welcoming me to work on getting their Congresswoman

Auschwitz

In Afghanistan as part of the Armed Forces
Parliamentary scheme

With the Body Scanners that
made the press

Doing my job, taken in Brussels parliament

'My first political caracuture'

With a Chinook helicopter during my training
with the Armed Forces Parliamentary Scheme

Shoulder to shoulder with local residents in Meriden fighting inappropriate development

Delivering food to food banks across the region. So far we've delivered over three tonnes

Meeting my employers with the mobile surgery in Leamington Spa

Talking to US Media on Obama's re-election, 2012

Leading an all-party delegation to Downing Street to hand in our historic 100,000 + petition

Watching Mo Farah achieve double Olympic gold success

Campaigning to save a West Midlands sport centre at Number 10

Still door knocking!

Petitioning to save a disabled riding centre

At the inaugural We Demand a Referendum Now conference

Meeting my idol Margaret Thatcher.

She told me to "never give up".

A very special moment

October 2008

Challenging the Prime Minister David Cameron about the need for a Referendum - September 2011

With UN Secretary General Ban Ki Moon June 2009

An honour to meet Her Majesty at a reception given for Parliamentarians at Buckingham Palace.

Image courtesy of British Ceremonial Arts Limited.

re-elected. I wouldn't be an employee, but they'd pay my expenses and I could work in their office.

The lawyers for the landlord went quiet. I flew to San Diego in the spring of 2002, knowing nothing about the place, and I loved it.

San Diego is a big military port, but this was before the Iraq war so that wasn't a distressing factor. I found all the resources of a city with none of the threats. I was about to settle in a third military town, but this one had a laid-back Californian vibe that Woolwich and Chatham had lacked.

The Democratic Representative in Congress was Susan Davis, a military wife with warm popular presence and a strong record of public service locally. She was good on the economy, education, women's rights and other causes dear to my heart and she was defending her seat for the first time. At first I just gave general assistance in the office and kept my eyes and ears open.

I found myself in a country where participation in the democracy is not a minority sport. The whole set-up favoured it: college students got a credit for helping with a political campaign and patriotism is part of being a citizen – you pledge allegiance to the flag every morning in American schools.

Susan Davis's campaign was expertly run. As the wife of a serviceman, she could claim the attention of Republican women. 'This guy' – meaning her opponent – 'doesn't understand what it means to be a military wife.' I learned new techniques; partly how to exploit new media, which was in its infancy, but mainly how to radiate a positive vibe. The difference in attitude is what struck me more than anything. Once you're used to American 'can-do-it'ness, both voters and politicians in Britain can seem diffident, apologetic, and as if they're enveloped in a permanent fog of despondency. American electioneering is overwhelmingly uplifting and cheerful.

The challenge for any politician is to create a clearly defined, assertive image in the minds of as many people as possible. Time is limited so the more focused your campaign the better. You draw attention to yourself; you hope the electorate is disposed to like you; and then – and this is the important part – you make a clear and memorable impression by consistently reiterating the same few points in all available media. Susan Davis was already well known and well liked, so our task was to make sure her loyal followers didn't feel over-complacent, and to hammer home to new voters the relevance of her message – especially as a military wife.

Once I'd been around for a while and was trusted, I could contribute to team discussions. It was a great campaign and Susan Davis got re-elected in November, 2002.

I was holding my own financially. My expenses covered most of my outgoings. With San Diego having been established in neighbourhoods isolated from one another by canyons, you drive everywhere. I rented a room in a house in North Park from an older lesbian couple who were very kind. I thought of them as my American moms, and bought myself a little car. I lived near Hillcrest, which is the main gay area. There's a gay centre there with support of every kind and I found it very easy to make friends. I loved it. I had a fantastic social life.

For a while after the election I simply went on working with the Democrats. I was now certain I wanted to be a politician in England. By meeting and networking I was able to get some paid work as a researcher, with conferences to go to in London, Frankfurt, Oslo, Prague and other European cities from which I would report back.

In the late summer of 2002, while I'd been working on Susan Davis's campaign, the Governor of California Gray Davis (no relation) had been re-elected after three years in office. He went on to make a number of unpopular political decisions. Most were liberal and went down badly with what in the US is called the middle class. (If you think middle-class in Britain, you think 'doctor in Sutton Coldfield'; if you think middle-class in America, you mean lower-middle, closer to 'primary school teacher in Coventry'.)

What Gray Davis lacked as a politician – aside from popular policies – was the all-important quality of chumminess. People like Bill Clinton and Boris Johnson have it in spades. Jimmy Carter and Nick Clegg, and as it turned out Gray Davis, have none at all. So in 2003 a Republican from San Diego, Darrell Issa, spotted an easy target and started a petition for the Governor's recall. A certain number of signatures are required to achieve a gubernatorial recall, which means automatic sacking.

I was on the ground collecting signatures for Darrell Issa's campaign, and the number was reached. This was only the second instance of such a recall in US history. And who would replace him? Issa, who poured a small fortune into his campaign, hoped that it would be him. But in the event, the recall merged into the election campaign begun by Arnold Schwarzenegger and became : 'Wouldn't you rather have Arnie instead of Gray?'

I learned a lot from helping with Issa's original signature campaign. Debates could get quite heated. Americans are more involved in their politics than the British, and more fiercely partisan. You had to engage, which I loved. Though most of this signature-getting was hard work, I was discovering much that was new to me. We didn't just go out armed with hope and a prayer. We were trained. We knew how to approach people, how to make our arguments and respond to challenges, how to give them written material and at what point to request a signature. It was impressed upon us that we were also building a database of sympathisers which would be useful in future. To some extent our pitch was scripted and choreographed like a telesales conversation, but the attitude I adopted in America – and for me it was reinforced in 2012 when I went to the US to help with the Obama campaign – was positivity.

'Oh,' people say to me in England, 'it must be really difficult being so tall. How d'you find clothes?' Or 'Don't you bang your head all the time?' or even, the corniest one of all 'Cold up there is it?'

In America they say 'Wow! Fantastic that you're so tall! You must get really noticed,' or 'Hey hey hey! I want you on my basketball team – you're so TALL! It must be brilliant for you.'

In America it's all about what you can do. In the UK we are all about what we can't do. As individuals we get knocked back very easily because in our minds we're already half-way there. I wish I could import American positivity. Living there instilled confidence in me. When I went there I'd worked for the Tories, and for UKIP, and was not without electioneering experience. I was used to knocking on doors, greeting the person who answered and beginning, in a conventional British whisper, head bowed:

'I'm sorry to disturb you', or 'I hope I haven't disturbed you'.

Immediately, I'd put myself in the wrong, and I'd made it worse, because they'd now be mildly irritated as they thought 'What's she want? If she was really sorry, she wouldn't have interrupted Eastenders.'

That kind of pseudo-politeness, this national obsession with apologising, is an error (and as I shall later explain, has a lot to do with our position on Europe). In the US we introduced ourselves and went right in with attention-grabbing urgency:

'We need to talk to you because this is important. We need your support.'

So it isn't what American campaigners do, but how they do it, that makes them so much more professionally adept than British campaigners. I took some UK staff with me to the Obama campaign and they are now among the most effective performers on my team. This is one of the things I love about America.

I was doing my freelance research projects and working on the Darrell Issa signature-collection, when I found myself working for the Schwarzenegger campaign. I met him twice briefly. 'VOW!' he said, in his Austrian-American accent: 'You're tall.' Of course this had been drawn to my attention before, but I guess it was an unusual thing for him to say. He has a huge presence, but he's shorter than you expect – about six foot.

I had to come back to London early in October, close to the end of his campaign, to attend the High Court. I was not represented, but I would speak for myself against UKIP's National Executive in the Chancery Division. My case was this: I was a paid up member and the constitution was a contract between me and the Party. By making a rule that contravened the Party Constitution prior to the election, allowing me to stand and be elected and then disqualifying me from the National Executive because I was an employee, they had applied their new rule retrospectively, and had been in breach of contract.

The hearing took place in one of the newer, blander, sound-deadened courts in the Royal Courts of Justice next to Aldwych. All I'd had to pay was a registration fee. I think it was £140.00. Mike Nattrass, the Deputy Leader, spoke for me. I stated my case. UKIP – represented by barristers, rather than in person – claimed in their defence that I had misread the Constitution. The key people in my disqualification were the Party's Returning Officer John de Roeck, and Michael Harvey the Party Secretary. I stayed in London for a week, waiting for the result, on tenterhooks, but also dying to get back to California for the gubernatorial election there.

I returned to court to find I'd won. And I was awarded about £9,500 in costs. As for the other side, they needn't be too bitter – their rule could stand from now, so no employee could be on the NEC.

I returned briefly to San Diego in time to see Gray Davis ousted and to rejoice with the team at Schwarzenegger's landslide victory: then I flew back to England. Thanks to that judgment in the Chancery Division, I was able to claim my seat on UKIP's National Executive. I had been elected for three years from late in 2001, so I had some time left and I devoted as much as possible to the NEC's preoccupations. We were all working towards the European Election of 2004.

But because being on the NEC was unpaid, I ended up putting

most of my hard-earned gains back into flying back and forth, paying rent in San Diego and Chatham, and giving time and energy to UKIP. I was passionate about it. But the Head Office moved from London to Birmingham that year, so travelling became a nuisance. As to ongoing business, Nigel Farage was now in dispute with John de Roeck and others, and wanted to get de Roeck out of the Party (a pattern was beginning to emerge).

I needed a job. I didn't yet have a Green Card to work in America, my income was non-existent in either continent and funds were dwindling. But in February of the Euro-election year I became Party Secretary. Ironically, because the NEC's rule on employees had been confirmed during the judgment against me, I would have to leave the NEC. I could live with that. I wasn't on the candidate list for Europe this time because I had been away when it was drawn up. UKIP did very well. Our single celebrity presence, Robert Kilroy-Silk, won one of the twelve UKIP seats and my friend Mike Nattrass became MEP for the West Midlands.

Mike promptly offered me a job as his political advisor in Birmingham despite Nigel Farage warning him not to employ me.

I couldn't have been happier.

20 | TAKING THE ENEMY'S SHILLING

I had a lot to thank Mike Nattrass for. He'd stood by me throughout all the problems I'd had with UKIP and was the only person in the Party to whom I'd confided the truth about my change of gender. And it was that summer, before I finally installed myself in Birmingham and took up my new job with him, that I was called in my capacity as Party Secretary by the journalist from the Telegraph, and I told that lie.

Mike and I discussed it when the article appeared. I told him I'd lied, and he didn't have to ask why – he understood the politics of it. He'd always said he admired my political brain, and now he said it again, which was comforting.

So everything looked good – though for the next five years I suffered from Alopecia and lost around 65 per cent of my hair. Doctors said it was the result of hormone treatment and stress.

I didn't know Birmingham at all. I rented the house of a friend who'd gone to New Zealand. It was in Halesowen, in the Black Country north of Birmingham, in a pleasant Edwardian cul de sac. In July I flew back to San Diego, packed up, sold my car, said goodbye to all my friends and moved back to the UK.

I was excited by my new job. I relinquished my Party Secretary role at the end of August and became Mike's second-in-command. My job was to be his eyes and ears in England while he was abroad, to collaborate with his team in Brussels and promote the Party's interests in the West Midlands by listening to constituents and bringing their problems to his attention. And of course to publicise every positive move he made. I was employed under contract to him through the EU. I loved it, and was busy all the time that winter.

My social life, on the other hand, was rubbish. It was dark at four o'clock and my evenings were spent alone. I'd spent a couple of mild winters on the Mexican-American border. Here, it was bitterly cold by November. There was a point where I thought 'what have I done?' I'd been living in Birmingham for nearly three months and I knew nobody: in San Diego I'd had about twenty friends I could have called. I thought I had made a huge mistake.

I'd reached my lowest point before Christmas when I met a woman, began a relationship and felt more at home in the Midlands.

The following May, the 2005 General Election took place. I stood as UKIP candidate for Halesowen and Rowley Regis. There was an important vote in the EU Parliament in January over the EU constitution, so I went to Brussels and unfurled a NO banner over the edge of the public gallery. Security men intervened, so in the end I held it above my head outside on the forecourt. Four or five of them punched me to the ground and dragged me along the ground. This was caught by an Italian film crew. Strangely, when it came to the investigation their film had gone missing, and the authorities denied that it had ever happened. Nigel said to me 'We don't want to make a big thing of this, Nikki.' Soon afterwards one of his assistants went on television and described how she had been pushed and she was distraught about it.

LGBT hustings were to be held in Birmingham, and UKIP was not invited; so I went along to protest about this and got arrested, which saw me featured on the front page of the Birmingham Mail. It didn't look like hard work, but it was. When support doesn't come from elsewhere, you have to raise your own profile.

Election day would be on Thursday, 5 May. On the Friday before, I got home to find a letter on the mat. My ex-landlord's solicitors in London had kept quiet for five years. They now informed me that unless I paid the outstanding £22,000 by the end of June, I would be made bankrupt.

There were many defeated candidates in the General Election. I lost my deposit by about seventeen votes. And sure enough, in July I was made bankrupt.

Mike was quite supportive, and the Party Secretary knew, but I discovered to my relief that bankruptcy – which had once meant three years of enforced penury and a ban on all sorts of activities, from directorships to public office – now lasted only a year, and was not so generally restrictive. I was employed, so I could make some payments. I had to have new bank accounts and so on, but my computer, car and other things which I needed for work remained my own. I had an interview with the Receiver and found the whole thing less painful than I'd feared.

I wondered what the landlord really got out of it. My bankruptcy was discharged in 2006. He had spent a lot of money and I'd learned a lesson. If I'd taken a stronger position in the first place, instead of simply withholding rent, I wouldn't have ended up in the mess I did.

My budding political career was unaffected, since I wasn't standing for political office at that time. As far as the press were concerned I was of no interest. Nobody brought up the subject until I had a public profile, and then it made no difference.

Mike Nattrass and I trusted one another. He had stood by me throughout all the problems I'd had with UKIP. But as year followed year, I got more and more frustrated with working for him. I wanted to implement ideas like mobile surgeries in the West Midlands, but he didn't want to deal with that level of effort. And there were other things. 2007 brought with it a summer of disastrously high rainfall all over England. From May to July the rain hardly stopped, and when Tewkesbury, a beautiful Gloucestershire town, was inundated and completely isolated, without clean water for 350,000 people, it made international news. Great swathes of Worcestershire were almost as badly affected, with deaths, motorway closures and the Severn and Avon overspilling their banks in numerous small towns. The whole West Midlands suffered badly.

The aftermath of a flood is squalor and sorrow. Filth pours into living rooms, cars and television sets and precious family photographs swirl away on the racing tide, pets drown, people have literally nowhere to go, and when the waters subside everything is smashed or lost; the emotional consequences can be post-traumatic stress and grief. The situation requires prompt action by insurers but in too many cases the insurers proved incompetent.

There is a European Disaster Fund for this sort of thing but it would be at least six months before it paid out. Mike was briefly at his home in England, while Parliament was closed for the summer. We had a short meeting at the UKIP office in Birmingham. I saw the political opportunity and advised him to get down to Worcester, where the Severn had flooded, and attack the EU for being so slow.

'Just to point out the facts,' I urged him. 'People don't understand that this is their own money. When you tell them we pay £52 million a day into the EU and we have every right to make an urgent claim – it'll make sense because they need that money. They're desperate. No other politician is telling them the truth.'

'Oh come on,' he said. 'The press won't take any notice.'

'Of course they will. It's a conflict. If journalists smell conflict they have a story. If our Government had kept the money the flood victims could have had it by now. It's perfect – pictures of you visiting, quotes from you asking why these people are being made to suffer when our own Government should have direct control of our own disaster fund.'

'It would be a waste of time anyway. It's nearly August. They'll all be away.'

'They are begging for news in August.'

Nothing I could say made any difference. He was about to leave for his villa in Portugal in a few days.

He went home and I walked upstairs to my office at the top of the building and literally banged my head against the wall. This was a wasted political opportunity. If he acted, the voters would understand, first, that a big share of the EU Disaster Fund was our money which – if we still had it – we could have distributed faster; and secondly, that this was UKIP, not any other party, agitating for immediate action.

I'd spent money, and scores of hours, on a leaflet campaign to say that UKIP was pushing for action from the Fund. This would score us 100 political points if the payout suddenly arrived – but my MEP wasn't pushing at all. Right now, he planned to laze on a vine-shadowed terrace with a glass of Douro and an airport blockbuster.

This, and other similar but less annoying instances, made me more than a little frustrated. So when by 2008 UKIP started to put together the internal list for the Euro elections of 2009, I decided to put my name forward.

I sailed through the West Midlands interview. The Lisbon Treaty was not being ratified – the Irish had said 'No' – and as a result the constituency had shrunk; we would have six people standing for election next summer, rather than seven as in the EU election of 2004. Mike was standing again. The long electoral process of weeding-out and testing opinion would go on for nine months before June, 2009.

Following the interview and the mandatory Criminal Records Check, in September 2008 there were hustings all over the region to decide which of the candidates would go forward for election. My main objective was to make sure that while I did well, Mike must come top of the list. There were two reasons for this. If only one UKIP candidate succeeded at the election next June, it was unlikely to be me, a first-time candidate – so all I would do, by fighting desperately for first place, was diminish Mike and allow someone else to come through the middle and win the single seat. I'd then lose my job as well as our friendship, which I valued highly despite my exasperation with him.

My second reason for thinking Mike would make a better lead candidate was that he would deflect any media scrutiny from me. In the hustings, therefore, most of my speeches were full of effusive regard for Mike and having been privileged to be part of all he had achieved.

Another candidate was Jill Seymour, whose husband was a major contributor to the campaign's finances. She really expected to come first. In the hustings 1200 people voted. Jill finished fourth, Mike first, and I came second. That autumn I was chosen to be Regional Chairman and Campaign Manager for the EU elections.

I was delighted. I knew we could do well. I had a strong position now; strong enough to put everything into place for a brilliant performance. All I needed was rather more tangible support than I'd learned to expect from Mike. But that autumn something extraordinary happened. There was to be a dinner at the Grosvenor House Hotel, in Park Lane, to celebrate the twentieth anniversary of the Bruges Group – the anti-Federalist group that had formed around Margaret Thatcher in 1988 when she refused any further transfer of power to Europe. I bought a ticket and went along hoping to meet Lady Thatcher, who would be there in her capacity as Honorary President.

The Ballroom was thronged with people clutching pre-dinner drinks and talking. I saw Nigel, who pretended not to see me, and a lot of other people I knew. I was in my element. Suddenly, ten yards away in the crowd, there was Lady Thatcher; security men following, cameras flashing. At 82, she was as elegantly-coiffed and made-up as ever, in a midnight blue dress. I couldn't help it; I pushed forward to be by her side and suddenly, there she was, listening as I told her she was my heroine and had inspired me to go in to politics. I went on to tell her what we were doing to get out of Europe. She seemed to admire my fighting spirit, and nodded approval as I spoke. Then she grabbed my hand and her eyes looked into mine. 'Never give up!' she said. 'Please, please, you must keep going! Never give up! Never give up!' She vanished among the crowd.

These were her people, still, years after she'd left Downing Street. I was overwhelmed and at the same time, I felt stronger. I wouldn't forget that. After all, I already had a history of not giving up. I was very pleased that it was reported in the BBC website and I was given a leading quote.

Re-motivated, I set about raising money and choreographing our campaign. I worked hard. I split up with my girlfriend. I still had a social life, but nothing would significantly distract me from where I was going politically.

All the same it was unlikely that I, as second on the list, would actually get elected. UKIP had done very creditably with 18% of the vote in 2004, and had only just missed out on having a second MEP. But now, with one seat fewer to play for, we needed something like 22%. There had to be a big swing to our views if we were to get it, but no-one was certain that the man and woman in the street were much more interested in Europe than they'd been five years before.

Then, only a few months before the election, Mike confided to me that he was going to remain an MEP for only half a term. When he stepped down, his seat would go to the next person on the list. So as long as he regained his seat, two and a half years from now I would become the MEP. Of course I agreed to that. Jill was told too. She was now Number Three on the list (the original Number Three having stood down), so if he and I were elected as MEPs, and he stood down at the end of 2011, Jill would replace him. He went on to reneg on this deal.

The hard part was waiting for the result. My parents were terrific support; in fact they'd helped me with the campaign – I couldn't want for more. They announced themselves proud of me. By this time, dad was a lot more cynical about the Labour Party, which in their twelve years in office had once again failed to prioritise the concerns of the working class. They seemed, if anything, to support big business. In 2009, this feeling wasn't unique to my dad. And it was the skilled working class – traditional Labour voters – who put UKIP in first place that year, in the Midlands towns which had been built on craft and industry like Stoke on Trent, Newcastle under Lyme, and Dudley.

On Sunday evening the results would be announced in Birmingham's National Indoor Arena. Mike Nattrass was soon sure that he'd retained his seat. When, around midnight, Dudley came up as a win I told all our supporters to give the biggest cheer – and they did; I couldn't stop grinning – we'd won. But at the very moment when all the TV cameras were pointing my way, shocking news arrived from the north-west: Nick Griffin, leader of the disgraceful British National Party, had been elected. A horror story and all the channels switched to cover it.

I delivered my speech regardless. I gave it all barrels and added something about the other parties being Fascists for ignoring the will of the people in not giving them a vote. This did not go down well with them, but all has been forgiven since

The following year I ran into Peter Skinner – the Labour MEP at the EU Parliament – who amazingly remembered me from my attack on him, as a student, in Strasbourg in 1997. The irony of my being a Member didn't evade either of us. He said he was appalled that I'd been thrown off that trip.

As a politician, you develop a sense of how harsh you can be before you overstep the mark into abuse. The aggressive interrogation to which I subjected Peter that day is pretty routine when we visit schools, and everyone knows politicians get heckled all the time. In the House of Commons, there's constant barracking, but you're not allowed to deliver a personal insult. In the EU Parliament the line between acceptable interrogation and damaging abuse varies widely between nationalities, although politicians who should know better have been known to say things for political effect at home. Nigel Farage insulted the President of the EU Parliament by remarking that he had the charisma of a bank clerk and came from a non-country. Farage was fined £4,000 for that and he certainly couldn't have bought so much publicity for the money. Presumably it didn't matter to him that he had also offended the entire population of Belgium and every bank teller in the world.

Peter and I are on friendly terms these days. We all mellow, with time, but I think voters are attracted to maverick politicians. Politicians have the big-Party line drilled into them. The Party ends up representing nobody. Any emotional response for or against a politician is a good thing. If you can't elicit an emotional response from your constituents, what are you doing?

Many people – including the Duke of Edinburgh, who I met at a recent Buckingham Palace reception – have asked why as a euro-sceptic I wanted to be a Member of the European Parliament. My answer is straightforward. I am in Brussels to represent the growing number of people who feel that they should not be subject to EU laws. I am there to help prevent harmful EU legislation impacting on our country. I do this in committee, predominantly the Employment and Social Affairs Committee, where my vote on amendments can be, and often is, a casting vote. It is far better for me to be in Brussels than a 'Lib-Lab-Con' MEP who seeks only EU consensus. As for UKIP, their MEPs rarely turn up for committees.

I'm also often asked about the 'gravy train'. So here goes my explanation.

As an MEP I am paid in euros as follows (figures are approximate).

Annual salary, €96,000 (current value about £85,000), plus €304 every time I sign in at Brussels; €4,300 a *month* for office administration costs and €21,4 a *month* for parliamentary assistants and other staff; and all accommodation and expenses paid for trips outside the EU, plus €4,300 a year for travel outside the UK.

Business class travel to all official Parliamentary meetings is refunded. The cost of most medical and dental care is refunded, I can claim up to €5,000 a year for language courses and up to €1,500 a year for IT training. I have a non-contributory pension from age 63 which is 3.5% of my salary for each year as an MEP.

It's an extremely important job. The laws I vote on affect everybody in the UK. I break the Working Time directive by putting in over seventy hours a week. Some other MEPs are equally diligent. But the vast majority are not. Why? Because they don't have to be.

There are 766 MEPs and we represent 28 countries. The 'office' for which administration costs are claimed – no receipts required – can be an MEP's own dining room table with a filing cabinet. Parliamentary assistants and other staff can be a spouse or working-age child. Do the words 'snouts' and 'trough' spring to mind? Or do you think we're worth every penny?

21 | UKIP – The Divorce

The European Union is in terminal decline. It is broken. All attempts at repair have so far failed. Given my view you might think it would be difficult to fall out with UKIP – but I managed it.

It wasn't the first time they'd got rid of me, but this time it was for good. I got kicked out around the New Year of 2010. I was, at the time, their third largest donor.

I had been elected the previous June: one of two UKIP MEPs for the West Midlands. Mike Nattrass, a businessman in his sixties, conformed to the general profile of those at the top of UKIP: white, male, benevolent, and a semi-retired businessman with an extremely healthy income.

UKIP was on the rise. The Party was only 16 years old, with a difficult (okay, sometimes disastrous) public profile. The average age of its members had always been far too high and as fringe parties do, it had attracted a few nutters and some swindlers in its time. It had begun with libertarian ideals but had gone through difficult periods in the late nineties with a lot of squabbling on the upper deck. I'd been there through most of this – in a subordinate role at the start, but for several years now as Mike's political advisor and as Campaign Manager for the region. I had risen in Mike's shadow, and in the summer of 2009, I appeared on UKIP's list of candidates for election to the European Parliament.

Until 1998 UKIP had considered that having an MEP was a conflict to its central aim of getting Britain out of the EU. But that year, at a party conference, Nigel Farage and others on the National Executive Committee pointed out that that if we did send MEPs to Brussels, we would get first-hand information about corruption and waste and how often the system faltered. I went there that day to vote against, and I ended up voting for; I was persuaded, mainly by the force of Nigel's arguments.

When UKIP regionally got 21.3% of the votes, I knew I was an MEP, with five years ahead of me in which to work for the cause. I was in shock. Delighted shock, of course, because I could now implement some of the many ideas which I had previously given up suggesting to Mike. Our share of the region's vote had gone up by about 3.5%, which was the highest increase in the country. Oddly, Nigel Farage's share of the vote in the south east had gone down by nearly 1%.

Nationally we ended up with 13 MEPs which was the same number as the Labour Party. The following day all the new UKIP MEPs were in London for a Press Conference. Afterwards we began talking about the upcoming Norwich by-election. We had to put in a strong appearance. How were we going to fund it?

I said: 'What's the problem? We're thirteen MEPs. If we each put in £3,000 that will pay for it.'

'You might be able to, but I've got a wife and kids to support,' Nigel snapped. I was astonished. So much for high ideals and promises about ploughing back our earnings to further the cause.

It was clear from the start that Nigel did not want me there. And that suspicion was confirmed in the next few days. I was told – though I can't swear that it's true – that someone called him to tell him I had been elected, saying 'Good news. Nikki's been elected.' He allegedly responded 'and you call that good news?'

Two others told me that Nigel – congratulated at the Press Conference about having thirteen MEPs – had muttered that he wished there were only twelve.

I'd known, deep down, that he was hostile, but this, tittle-tattle or not, was still hurtful. Margaret Thatcher had been my role model since I was ten, but I now understood the famous speech Howe had made

– about going off to play cricket only to find that your bat has been broken before the game by the team captain.

I had never been among Nigel's in-crowd, but there hadn't been open sniping either. I was UKIP's answer to Labour's John Prescott – an embarrassment that the leadership tolerated as the token representative of his Party's fundamental ideals. Only Prescott, of course, had powerful sources of funds behind him.

Life has given me a very thick skin and the ability to hang onto my ideals when all around me others are losing theirs. Whatever happened, I'd won this job – and as campaign manager I'd worked for it. I was going to carry on doing all I could to serve the voters by getting us out of Europe.

The EU Parliament, being so big and so various, operates by being divided into Groups. In Groups, Members from participant national parties, with roughly similar aims, meet and agree on the views they'll unite to express in Parliament. UKIP delegates were expected to sign up to a Group called Independence and Democracy, so I did.

Independence and Democracy still existed at the time, but only just. A bunch of leading Italians from Lega Nord – Berlusconi supporters – had been thrown out for wearing the notorious Danish cartoon of Mohammed on their T-shirts. This satisfied Nigel Farage and UKIP, three protesting Swedes and several others, but left them with too few members to carry on. You need 25 members in a Group or you don't get any EU funding.

Groups get EU money, did I forget to say? And if they have 30 members and above, they get considerably more. Like much of of the money paid to individual MEPs this is supposedly to be used for EU purposes.

UKIP was about to quit Independence and Democracy, leaving it unfunded for lack of support, and therefore non-existent.

This opened a whole new can of worms for me.

Farage had been a prime mover in Independence and Democracy. Now he could either take us into some sort of union with the far right, or go with the more moderate Group headed up by the British Tories. A couple of weeks after the Euro-elections, the Conservatives had left Europe's biggest centre-right Group, the EPP, and formed a new one called European Conservatives and Reformists. It was anti-federalist, as we were, and had over fifty members from eight countries already.

So Farage had choices – not go with a Group at all; go with the Conservatives and Reformists (which he would have no chance of leading); or go with some of the extremists he'd already helped to throw out of Independence and Democracy. Lega Nord had done very well in the Italian elections. They had ten seats. UKIP had thirteen. Twenty-three, then; add in a couple of Danes, a Dutch MEP and a few more, call them the European Group for Freedom and Democracy (EFD) – and he'd scrambled together a well-funded group of thirty members of which he could be Chairman.

I was asked to sign up. And the deadline was 14 July.

I was unhappy since I knew all about Lega Nord. It wasn't just that they were in favour of the Lisbon Treaty – a huge step towards a Federal Europe that would come into force a few months from now. The immediate problem was a man called Mario Borghezio, notoriously fond of raising his arm in a Fascist salute. I learned he had criminal convictions for violence towards a minor and for setting alight immigrants' belongings when they were asleep in a doorway. A frequent guest on Borghezio's radio show was Father Abrahamowicz; they concurred in their belief that Auschwitz was nothing more than a 'cleansing chamber'. The Lega Nord Mayor of Treviso verbally promoted ethnic cleansing of Treviso's homosexuals and the whole Party hated gypsies. Bossi, their esteemed leader, had said he wanted to shoot at African refugees as they landed in Italy from boats.

I loathed and despised this shower and everything they stood for. I did not want to share a conference room with them, never mind an alliance.

168

I believed that, for the sake of UKIP's image, the coherence of its policies, and its future membership profile, the Party should not go anywhere near them.

When I first raised my objections with Mike Nattrass he looked dismayed.

'Oh, you're not going to cause any trouble, are you?'

Meaning, trouble within UKIP. Later when I found I'd missed discussions about the new Group, I thought I'd been deliberately sidelined – I had not been consulted and decisions had been made in my absence. At the start of the first week in July, Members from all over Europe had joined UKIP and Lega Nord in the EFD.

But only 29 of them. And time was running out

22 | THE NAUGHTY STEP

I now took my first step towards expulsion: I refused to join the EFD.

Mike was urging me to sign up. I had dug in my heels. And Nigel was refusing to speak directly to me at all. Mike, on the phone on Sunday night, before the critical deadline, sounded dismayed.

'You've made your point. Just go in first thing and sign on Tuesday, Nikki, for god's sake. Make Nigel happy – Wednesday's cutting it too fine,' he said.

'As things stand I will not be signing. If he wants to discuss it get him to call me.'

I was already exhausted from the pre-election campaign but I somehow kept going at full speed. I was travelling to Belgium and back every other week, and in between gathering even more paperwork, setting up offices and finding staff in Brussels and Birmingham, talking to Mike and looking for an apartment in Brussels. I still hadn't explained my position to Nigel. I understood that he needed to lead a united Party, but I thought UKIP must recognise (as the other Parties do) that individuals have a right to take a moral stand.

But his tactic was avoidance.

Late on the Monday night the phone rang in my hotel room. I paraphrase the conversation we had.

'What's all this nonsense?'

'It isn't nonsense Nigel. It's a matter of principle.'

'Nikki. We all know you're wonderfully high-minded, but it is not possible for UKIP to survive without joining a Group. Maybe

171

individual members do have dubious views, I wouldn't know. Sometimes we have to compromise as even you will probably learn, when you've been here long enough.'

'UKIP's constitution says we can link up with like-minded people anywhere in the world, yeah? But they're not like-minded. They're racists and anti-Semites, they support Berlusconi...'

'So you say.'

'These people are nutters – that's why you kicked them out before. And they support the Lisbon Treaty!'

'First of all, you haven't proved to my satisfaction that they've done any of the things you say. Secondly, as a Group we won't support the Treaty. No problem there.'

'You don't think their views are a problem?'

'Look. We can talk about all this later. Whenever you like. Right now, we are hours from the deadline. I don't have very much time.'

'I believe there's something called being non-inscrit? I can do that; just secede and still represent UKIP in everything else.'

'That is not an option for you.'

A Member can be non-inscrit if their Party respects their reasons for not being part of the Group and wants to keep them on-side. Nigel said:

'Listen, I have taken time out to call you and I don't have time to argue about your views. I've got a breakfast in the morning with influential people. You are seriously mistaken, Nikki, if you think that as a recently-elected Member you can just take it into your head to cost the Party half-a-million pounds.'

How much? I was too staggered to say anything.

'Because if you do, I'll let everyone know about it. I can safely say your reputation will suffer.'

I took this to mean that he would finish my political career before it started. Unless I did as he said.

'Are you still there?'

'Yes.'

'Right. I have to go. I have to go now. I simply want your assurance that you will sign in the morning.'

'I will if you promise to talk to me about this. I want you to know how serious it is for the Party.'

'Yeah, yeah, of course. Trust me, we'll talk it through and work out a better way forward.'

So the following morning, I signed.

Afterwards I burned with shame. My first act, on becoming an MEP, had been to cave in. So much for sticking to my principles.

I parked the remorse. I was elected, I could do things, I could push the cause along. I had all this energy and a million and one ideas that Mike Nattrass had been reluctant to implement.

I'd thought this moment would never come and now it was here. For a couple of decades, I'd thought it impossible that I'd ever be a politician. And now I had five years in which to prove myself. I could show how good I could become at this job. I wanted to make UKIP mainstream, not a party whose image attracted only old people and eccentrics. We had a General Election coming up next year and a lot of my plans were about how we were going to fight it. My idea was to target certain seats and oust the Liberal Democrats from the whole West Midlands. Mike had been dubious. Not really sure if we could. I'd kept arguing: 'If we attack them accurately, we can do it. And then, when they pop up being interviewed about Europe, we can ask the BBC why they are talking to the Lib Dems when they are not even represented in this region.'

This fell on deaf ears. I took a much needed, two-week holiday in

San Diego, and admitted to myself that fundamentally, UKIP was badly run. Most of the senior people were very successful businessmen: very probably millionaires, and all men. But UKIP was their hobby. They cared a lot, but implementation was not their thing. Mysteriously, finances were their weakest point. Had the main players acted in business with the same lack of energy they gave to UKIP they'd all be scraping a living. UKIP had no business plan, no economic plan, and no cost-benefit analysis. And this was in 2009 when it had been going for sixteen years.

There had been an upsurge in membership in 2004 which had caused a lot of controversy about its finances. UKIP had a rule: if a branch attracted a new member, the members' subscriptions stayed in branch for the first year, but Head Office took the renewal subs. Maybe not financially terribly sound, but that was the rule. And the EU Parliament Member did not need to live in the area of the branch; if the member was attracted to the branch, that's where the money stayed for a year.

So the south east area, where Nigel Farage was standing in 2004, set up a call-centre in Ashford, Kent, phoned people and sold them five-year subscriptions. It's frequently alleged within the Party, though I don't know if it's true, that these funded Nigel's election campaign. None of the money was ring-fenced and the central Party had to finance those memberships for five years, including the first: all the magazines, and all the internal ballots, which cost money. Yet no money had been put aside for this.

Imagine a cosy, charming, indefinably provincial city where several mega-buildings, all shiny, new and different, have landed from outer space. Along with a vast multi-national population to fill them. That's Brussels. The European Parliament is unmissable; glass, vaguely eighties in design, and post-modern; besides the enormous almost-circular debating chamber, there are many similar mini-debating chambers for Groups of 25 upwards, and for Committees – such as Human Rights, Civil Rights and Women's Issues, all of which I joined.

They accommodate both participants, translators and assistants. Besides these there are dozens of meeting rooms, offices, foyers, ante-chambers, atria, restaurants, store-rooms, staff canteens, security, telecoms, utility cupboards, switchboards...

Unwieldy does not begin to describe it.

I moved into an apartment, fought my way up from under the deluge of reports, round robins and guidance notes and attended my first meeting of the European Group for Freedom and Democracy. I met other members. One was a tall blond Dane with wide, blue eyes called Morten Messerschmidt who had a conviction for inciting racial hatred. Two members of a Greek Party led by Karatzaferis, had challenged the Israeli Ambassador in Athens to come and debate the 'Auschwitz and Dachau myth'. They appeared to think that 9/11 was a Jewish plot as well.

Uncomfortable does not begin to describe my feelings. I remembered the school visit by a survivor of Treblinka. I had never felt so moved. You don't forget that.

And now, to be sitting in this room, linked to these people, was vile.

We also had informal meetings of the UKIP MEPs, chaired by Nigel as Party Leader. One meeting I remember particularly well.

We were supposed to be talking about finances, specifically how to spend the money we were being given for EU business. I told the meeting that as I'd joined some Committees, I needed assistance. This request led to a wider discussion about how our EU funding should be spent, and what UKIP had to pay for. It was slightly diverted into a discussion on exactly where the Group's money went. I understood by now that the EU funding that goes into a Group is supposed to be devoted to the business of the Group – which in the case of EFD, was opposing the Lisbon Treaty and federalism in general.

But I had a few more detailed questions about UKIP's money.

Nigel got furious.

'I'm not discussing that. I'm telling you.'

I said 'Hang on a second, we're supposed to be discussing finances, and I have these questions.' I had been briefed by one of my researchers and began to put some queries which were not specific, but which did not elicit a straight answer. I wanted to know what the money was being devoted to. Would we see accounts?

I got dismissive answers, but I kept pushing.

Then – I think it was when I asked about the accounts – Nigel flipped. His fist thundered onto the table in front of me. I felt the rush of air past my face and jerked away from the table. Afterwards I was trembling.

'Will you just stop it!' he screamed. 'You are interrupting the meeting, you are interrupting me, and if you don't stop I'll ask you to leave.'

No-one said a word. I just sat there, shocked.

Nigel resumed the meeting. I left at the end. I was a new MEP and I thought the way the party was run was important.

Mike Nattrass was back in England, but I told him about it. When he came back he said: 'Nigel says he just can't talk to you.'

'But he needs to apologise. He's Party Leader. He should be briefed to deal with questions like this.'

'Well...'

Rumours then began to spread about me; one of my advisors – who had formerly been one of Nigel's assistants, but had fallen out with him – was said to be an MI6 agent. This, it was alleged, was why I had queried UKIP's finances. My staff had been infiltrated by MI6, and I should be ignored.

Oh well. At least I was part of a pattern of undermining that I recognised from the book Animal Farm. As a daring subversive in our circle – at least that's how I felt I was increasingly seen – I suspected it was the only novel our Leader had ever read, and which he had used as an instruction manual for running the Party.

Nigel's favourite slurs were: 'closet BNP!' (which was one thing he knew he couldn't smear me with) and 'MI6 infiltration!' And madness of course ('Don't listen to anything she has to say – she's unhinged.')

I was an enemy of the State, apparently.

September was the month of the Party Conference in Southport. There was plenty of heartening self-congratulation about gains we'd made at the European elections, and much Tomorrow The World bluster.

But then Nigel Farage resigned as Party Leader. This came out of the blue. He told his crestfallen audience that only pressure of work forced him to desert us at this, our hour of triumph. He reminded us that he was already a Group Leader in Brussels, an MEP and Party Leader. He intended to be a serious candidate for our side in the 2010 General Election, and therefore had no choice but to sacrifice the leadership.

Since he was going to fight John Bercow, the Speaker of the House of Commons, in Bercow's Buckinghamshire constituency, the more cynical among the audience thought he'd no chance of winning and wanted to disassociate the Party from failure. The Speaker is normally unchallenged, so Farage standing against him would attract a lot of media attention whatever the result. His argument was that this would publicise the Party.

On the other hand – he could have resigned as Group President. After all, UKIP's position is that what happens in Brussels is less important than what happens in the UK.

But I later discovered that his resignation, far from being impromptu and a shock to all, had been quietly prepped. The night before, he'd phoned Lord Pearson, a respected member of the House of Lords, as well as an active UKIP supporter and told him: 'I'm going to resign.' Lord Pearson told me later that he had desperately tried to talk him out of it. Nigel suggested that Pearson would be the perfect substitute. 'Absolutely not!' came the appalled response. But our Leader knew how to play people.

So Nigel made his shocking announcement at the conference. Pearson immediately climbed onto the dais with an air of high drama.

'I demand, Nigel, that you WITHDRAW that resignation!' (Self-effacing murmurs, and a shaking of the head from Farage.) Come on everybody! We DEMAND that Nigel Farage remains our Leader!'

The audience of about 1,200 people rose to their feet (those who could, anyhow) and clapped and roared. With mournful tread, Nigel walked down steps from the dais and made his way towards the back of the room. Clasping hands, touching shoulders, comforting weeping old ladies, he slowly progressed up the central aisle, past his adoring fans – circumnavigated the entire audience from the back of the room and along the front row and disappeared into the VIP room with Lord Pearson crying in broken falsetto:

'Nigel, Nigel! Withdraw, withdraw!'

Nigel reappeared. His lower face is deeply furrowed, reminding me of a Danish pastry, and kind of slides seamlessly into his neck. My inner granny looks at Nigel and thinks 'You should'a bin on the Halls.' He was born just a hundred years too late. So it's hard to say when he's truly regretful, but he certainly looked serious on this occasion.

'Sometimes you have to be strong about these things. Sometimes you have to be strong and make the right decisions.'

After that it all went like clockwork. Lord Pearson put himself forward as leader and other candidates were invited to stand.

I mischievously set up an online petition, shrilly demanding 'Nigel must stay! We need Nigel!' I got a nasty letter from him. This must stop. Immediately. For some reason he thought I was not entirely sincere.

David Campbell Bannerman, Gerard Batten and Mike Nattrass stood for the leadership and so did I, though I didn't expect to win. But I thought I might be able to make some changes just by standing – producing ideas and implementing them.

In my speech to conference I announced that I was going to give one-third of my post-tax salary as an MEP directly to the Party. Annually, for five years.

It is illegal for MEPs to spend their EU funding on Party politics. But nobody can tell us what we can do with our net salary, and for every day that I sign on in Brussels I get 304 euros tax free. So to devote £20,000 from post-tax salary to promoting the Party is achievable. If all thirteen UKIP MEPs did the same the Party would be £260,000 better off every year. By demonstrating such commitment, I reasoned, UKIP would be more likely to attract big donors.

My fellow MEPs were tight-lipped, but my speech was well received. I'd been in the Party for a long time and people knew my name. They knew how hard I worked; I had a reputation as a maverick, but people like that in a politician. The Party disliked it because I could not be controlled.

So I put myself forward and held my own. I got on quite well with Pearson. I'd already put out a leaflet about my first hundred days as an MEP, and all the things that I had done with the staff and resources I was given; we'd produced and distributed throughout the West Midlands, a sixteen-page newspaper in the first month and had, effectively, carried on campaigning. UKIP had stopped after the European election, but I thought we should keep the pressure up because we would have a General Election to fight next year.

In my Leadership Manifesto I set out what I'd do in my first hundred days as Party Leader. I wanted a Leader's Question Time twice a month, when Party members could ring up and ask questions directly. I wanted a policy manual, a business plan, a commitment to transparency and properly audited accounts from every MEP. I promised to put Nigel Farage at the centre of the Party where he belonged. (We're all allowed just one big lie in exceptional circumstances.)

Everyone thought these ideas were wonderful. Lord Pearson certainly did, and I led in the online leadership campaign.

Had I won, I could have withdrawn UKIP from the EFD. And I could have insisted that MEPs use their staff in a more productive way. In my experience at that point, other MEPs didn't give their people enough to do. If ideas were lacking, I could provide plenty.

During the campaign Nigel Farage had been interviewed on BBC TV. He told Andrew Neil that Lord Pearson was 'the only credible candidate'.

Gerard Batten and I challenged him about this later, when we were all in Brussels. He said:

'Well make a complaint about it. Fucking chuck me out of the party.' In the end Pearson won, Gerard came second and I was voted third.

Throughout this time, before and after the Party Conference in November that year, other issues were live, such as whether or not we should form a Pan-European Party. The Greens were in one and so were Labour, the Lib-Dems and the Tories.

There was more money in belonging to a Pan-European Party. These are entities in which not only MEPs but Members of Parliament and (for instance) Members of the London Assembly can participate. They are a clear step along the road to the EU Parliament having Parties of its own; in other words, a move towards federalism and a further weakening of the nation state.

After the Conference, at a UKIP meeting in Strasbourg, Nigel proposed that we form a Pan-European Party along with the EFD. However, a brisk decision was called for.

'We've only got days to sign up! And if we don't sign up we'll lose all this money – €900,000.'

A babble of enthusiasm arose.

'Hang on a second,' I said. Icy stare from Farage. I pointedly addressed the others. 'This is for the membership to decide. Especially since Nigel's now resigned the leadership. This is for the new Leader!'

Silence.

Fortunately Trevor Colman, the MEP for the South West, spoke up. He agreed that this key decision should be put to the party members. So the proposal to join a Pan-European Party was not signed that day, and I leaked it to the membership; some of whom started questioning their own MEPs; who then started saying: 'Oh no, we're opposed to it.' Cowards.

That autumn, Fabian Olins my very good friend died. He was a volunteer in the London Head Office and one of my biggest supporters. He titled himself 'The humble toiler in the vineyard'. When he thought I was wrong he would privately tell me so, but he would go out and defend me to the hilt. I'm glad he saw me elected before he died.

I had become a thorn in UKIP's side. And Nigel Farage was starting to wince when I crossed his field of vision.

But I was still trying to talk to him because I was so unhappy about being in the EFD. I wanted to leave – effectively, to be non-inscrit. If all else failed I would be 'unattached', the equivalent of an Independent in the British political system. I had discussed the mechanics of this with Edward McMillan-Scott, who has been an MEP for years, and works tirelessly for Human Rights. A Liberal Democrat MEP now, he'd resigned as a Conservative MEP because he was repelled by the toxic right-wingers they were sitting with in the ECR Group.

I pushed for a meeting with Nigel before Christmas, when we'd all be at Strasbourg for a Plenary Session, and it happened at last. Face-to-face, we sat together one afternoon, under strip lights in a windowless meeting room.

What followed was acrimonious. Again, I paraphrase most of this.

'You seem to have some difficulty with authority figures. Might I remind you that I'm Group Leader, and you're not?' Nigel said.

'This is a matter of principle.'

'Nikki how many more times? You represent the Party here; you therefore must be in the Group.'

'So you say. But Lord Pearson is Leader. I've already told him what I think of the EFD and he says he doesn't care whether I'm in a Group or not, as long as I carry on with all the work I do to promote the Party in the West Midlands. He likes my ideas.'

'That idiot Pearson doesn't know what he's talking about.'

'Oh? I thought he was the only credible candidate.'

Sharp intake of breath. 'You have too much to hide.'

'What?'

'Well, for one thing, you've been a bankrupt.'

'So? I was perfectly open about it.'

'You didn't disclose it to the Party,' he said. 'That's a clear breach of Party rules.'

'Mike Nattrass knew about it and so did the Party Secretary! Mike was Deputy Leader. Ask Zuckermann, he was Party Secretary, he advised me about it. If anybody didn't disclose it, it wasn't me.'

'I have asked Michael Zuckermann. He says he knew nothing. '

'Of course he did.' (I asked Michael afterwards; he's a lawyer, and he said something about client confidentiality.)

'And you've lied to journalists.'

'I what? When?'

'When they asked you about a personal matter.'

Light dawned. 'Oh.'

I knew what he was talking about. How low could this man go?

'The position is as follows. If you stay in the EFD, you stay in the Party. If you don't you will no longer represent UKIP. And you'll be unattached. Sitting up there in the Chamber next to the BNP.'

'You don't get it. I'm not going to be bullied. I'd rather get out.'

'I suppose you want the extra money.'

I was speechless. We were all afloat on money. What I would need, as an unattached MEP, would be time, to do stacks of preparatory reading myself – because I wouldn't have access to the pool of researchers who supplied information to Party members. How dare he –

'Right,' he said. 'You'll find yourself sitting next to Nick Griffin then. Enjoy.'

I seceded from the Group and promptly got suspended from UKIP by the National Executive Committee of the Party (in the absence of Lord Pearson, who claimed that he had to speak at an important House of Lords debate).

When I returned to the European Parliament at the beginning of January 2010, I presented my letter of resignation to Jerzy Buzek, the President of the European Parliament. From then on, I became 'unattached'.

23 | SERVING MY EMPLOYERS

I didn't end up sitting next to Nick Griffin. The chamber of the EU Parliament is arranged in a horseshoe, and all the unattached members are clustered at the back. I make sure to maintain an Exclusion Zone many seats wide between myself and the BNP man.

I wasn't a UKIP MEP but I was still much too closely identified with them by the West Midlands electorate. And I still stood, on the whole, for the same founding principles that UKIP had, only with more fervour.

I was a maverick in UKIP, but on my own, I could only be effective by clarifying my own unwritten constitution, principles and rules. In the early months of 2010 I defined exactly what these were so that I could follow my own Party line at all times. I would always be willing to change my opinion if circumstances change, but in general, I put the facts alongside my principles and decide which line I will take. So I have learned to select my causes according to my beliefs – in self-determination, human rights, and equality of opportunity. But the General Election of May, 2010, reminded me that I was still attached in the public mind to UKIP. I had to define a separate brand identity. What, realistically, could I achieve for my constituency that UKIP couldn't?

We were now to be governed by a coalition of Liberal Democrats and Conservatives. I sat down and read the Coalition's programme for Government. Two statements jumped out at me:

We will ensure that any petition that secures 100,000 signatures will be eligible for formal debate in Parliament.

The petition with the most signatures will enable members of the public to table a bill eligible to be voted on in Parliament.

185

This was new and it was right there in black and white and, while noting that 'eligible for' didn't mean 'would qualify for', I trusted that it would be implemented. At the core of my feeling about the EU is the arrogance with which we were bundled into membership in the first place. We were not asked. We should be asked. Suppose my team and I were to organise a campaign to collect 100,000 signatures demanding a referendum on whether we should stay in, or leave, the EU?

Certainly 100,000 signatures would get a lot of publicity. People all over the country would have the opportunity to tell Downing Street exactly how they felt. If it was going to get taken seriously it'd have to be cross-Party, and that would identify me in the public mind as separate from UKIP.

It would mean a lot of work. If every one of ten thousand supporters brings ten friends to sign, you have 110,000 signatures. You've spread the circle of influence. I thought about the recall election in California that Arnold Schwarzenegger ultimately won. I would have to get my team in the Midlands just as enthusiastic as I'd been in San Diego and suggest some signature-gathering techniques. Right now I was too busy (we all were), so we postponed the launch of our 'WE DEMAND A REFERENDUM' campaign until August, 2010.

One hundred thousand is an easy number to say, but it doesn't really explain the level of work required, the amount of time it takes and the dedication it demands. We wrote to everyone on our database, we had our mobile surgery (a converted camper van) and from that autumn until the following summer we drove around the West Midlands listening, talking and collecting signatures on our petition in market-places and village halls. The reaction was overwhelming. Supporters we'd never even met spent whole evenings tramping from door-to-door. A woman in North Wales got about 4,500 signatures and a heroic gentleman on the south coast collected around 6,000. My wonderful mum got about 3,500. It was a startling example of people power.

Mike Nattrass and another UKIP MEP, Trevor Colman, had now had enough of Farage's insistence that UKIP remain in the vile EFD Group. They too became non-inscrit and used some of their own funding to help us. Thanks in part to them, we were able to advertise in the Daily Mail, Daily Telegraph and The Sun. The postbags of responses were bulging; they had to be heaved off the van and onto the office floor. The staff were spending all day just opening envelopes. The campaign was snowballing.

We were pipped at the post for 'first ever debate inspired by popular petition' by another one demanding action on the injustice over what had happened at Hillsborough. Given my personal experience of this tragedy, and my enduring hero-worship of Kenny Dalglish who'd supported the Hillsborough petition, I didn't mind at all.

But one day early in August, 2011, we were able to announce that we had 100,000 signatures. Infuriatingly, our press coverage was overwhelmed by the maelstrom of the London riots which kicked off that day. But when we delivered our petition to Downing Street on Thursday, September 8, signatures were still rolling in and we were certain we could force a debate. Photographs show us flanked by Labour MPs Kate Hoey and Kelvin Hopkins. Other MPs joined them in supporting the petition.

David Nuttall, MP, sponsored the petition in the Back Bench Business Committee and a Commons debate was scheduled for 27th October 2011. The Foreign Office would of course be concerned with the demand for a Referendum on Europe, so William Hague, the Foreign Secretary, should attend. In the end, because of commitments in Australia by Hague and the Prime Minister, the debate was brought forward to the previous Monday.

It marked the first time that a public petition had brought the Prime Minister to the dispatch box. On the day, we delivered a further 21,000 signatures to Downing Street. Feeling in the West Midlands ran highest of all, with 53,000 of the total.

The debate was heavily whipped, with the Coalition of course encouraging their Members to vote against. All the same, we won over 111 MPs, including 81 Conservative rebels. Two Parliamentary Private Secretaries resigned over it, saying that the Coalition Whip demanded that they vote against democracy which, as a matter of conscience, they refused to do.

Outside on College Green, broadcast journalists were interviewing all the usual suspects. I was exultant, feeling that we'd created history. But I was astonished to see Nigel Farage, of all people, ranting to a TV reporter about how remarkable an indication of public feeling this was. He'd refused to sign on several occasions. In fact a letter from his Brussels office had informed a constituent that such petitions were a waste of time.

So I pushed myself alongside him and in firm but softly spoken tones pointed out that since he had previously refused to sign he might wish to do so now. I shoved the paperwork into his hands and with a camera pointed at him, he scrawled his name.

Later that night, on BBC News, I was asked where we would go from here. I made it clear that I was never going to give up; that we would keep collecting even more signatures so that we'd gain the right to table a Bill. We did – our grand total, collected between 2010 and 2012, was about 200,000, of which 74,000 were from West Midlands voters. This is when it became evident that the phrase 'will enable members of the public to table a bill' actually meant 'will not necessarily enable members of the public to table a bill.' Because despite what the Coalition's programme for Government had said, they wouldn't let us take the issue any further.

At the Tory Party conference that year I happened to come face to face with David Cameron. I strongly put the case for a In-Out EU referendum. He was charming but told me that he felt Britain's place was in the EU and that we should renegotiate from within. Unfortunately there wasn't time, then, to debate that critical point.

But the petition campaign succeeded as a demonstration of the strength of public opinion. It wasn't me alone who did that. My staff worked tirelessly on the organisation. People up and down the country spent their own time to valuable effect. And those who simply signed the petition showed their belief in the importance of democracy. I am immensely proud of all of them.

I felt I had brought coherence to a tangled task in my first twelve months as an MEP. Throughout that year I found Lady Thatcher's words 'Never Give Up' had often echoed in my mind.

Nowadays I usually find myself dealing with social problems that are only obliquely associated with the main argument about Europe. Domestic debt is high on the list. My staff has managed to sort out well over a quarter of a million pounds' of constituents' personal debt. Usually people come to us after they've had no luck approaching their Members of Parliament. We get their creditors to agree that the sum can be paid off slowly and steadily – even at one or two pounds a week. And I've lost count of the number of people we have rehoused.

Asda allowed us to set up a trolley in their branches with a request that people donate some spare groceries to it, and we've been able to deliver more than three tons of food to food banks. Then there is the controversial Pay Day app on your phone will offers a payday loan in about thirty seconds, but will charge interest of up to 1000 per cent. This is a short-cut to destitution, social control masquerading as generosity.

Holding people to account on issues like this is a big part of my work. So I visited one of the payday loan companies. It's an outfit that tells people they can afford a 42-inch plasma TV and a leather sofa on income support. I asked the Board to tell me the legal definition of income support. None of them knew. It is the minimum amount you need to live on. They said 'Thank you. We will review our plans.' I have yet to hear from them. I did, however, secure compensation for the cases I brought to their attention.

At present there is nothing, legally, that can be done about companies like that. There should be, but not only is our government supine in the face of such outrage, so is the EU.

I have to deal directly with concerns at home and abroad which means switching between them with the facts at my fingertips. I can only do this with the support of good researchers behind me.

Some issues are important to all my constituents, and others – like the desperate political situations in Kashmir and Cyprus – affect only minorities.

The 2014 EU election approaches and I want to raise the profile of WE DEMAND A REFERENDUM NOW – Still further, especially in the West Midlands. Fortunately I have a strong team based in Birmingham and another in Brussels. The home team organise publicity, newsletters and booklets, and set up my travelling surgery-cum-roadshow. They book space and time at county shows, market days and village fetes. I drive around in my colourfully emblazoned Mini and speak and hold regular surgeries at places I visit. You'd think, given the state of the economy, that all MEPs would be doing this, but I am the only one.

24 | BLIP

The phone rang at 7.30 in the morning. The caller said he was a Detective Inspector from West Midlands Police.

'Are you at home?'

'No. I'm on my way to Brussels. What's this about?'

'We'll call you back in five minutes.'

'But –'

'We'll call you back.' They rang off.

I was exasperated. If there'd been a burglary why didn't he say so? I often drive to and from Brussels and I had spent the night in a hotel near the British end of the Channel Tunnel. I needed to get my car onto the train in the next hour. It was February 2012, still dark, and I was in a hurry.

He called back. 'We have a warrant to search your house.'

'What? Why?'

'I can't tell you that. You need to be here.'

'I'm supposed to be in Brussels.'

'If you have to go to Brussels for your work, then so be it. But I would advise you to come home.'

'Please tell me why?'

'I'm not prepared to tell you on the phone.'

'I've got to make a value judgement here. To carry on with my duties in Brussels or turn back. Is this about a driving with a bald tyre, or murder? Where along that line?'

He hesitated. 'It's concerned with your mandate.'

That meant my term as an MEP. 'Right,' I said. 'I'll be there.'

On the way home I phoned my solicitor and asked him to call the police. I did not have to go to my house. We would meet at his office and go to the police together, voluntarily.

We walked into the police station. The caller had not informed me that they had two other warrants: one to search my office and another to arrest several members of my staff. Nor that I would be placed under arrest for conspiracy to defraud.

The accusations were that:

I had misclaimed travel allowances. (**KERCHING!** I knew where this was coming from.)

I was paying bonuses to my staff that they were expected to pay back.

It is now November 2013, twenty-one months since these events, and although my staff were released without a stain on their characters, I am still on police bail.

Here's what actually happened. In July or August, 2009, when I became a UKIP MEP, a man started working for me in UKIP's Birmingham office. Let's call him 'Faustus'.

I took him with me to Brussels that August. I'd been a Member for about six weeks and the European Parliament building had just re-opened for business after the summer break. The idea was that when I communicated with Faustus, back in Birmingham, he'd be familiar with where I was working, as well as key individuals I was working with, and would understand the process of presenting data to the EU. He would be dealing with staff contracts, infrastructure, and travel – as well as acting as liaison between me and my constituents and advising me on the political situation at home.

But within the first few months, I began to see him as a bit of an idiot. As my political advisor, at a time when I was in conflict with

UKIP's Party leadership, he kept on urging me to leave UKIP and 'start my own party.' Well thanks, I thought. Fantasy wasn't really a big help at the time. But worse than this, he was disruptive. Two other members of staff were undermined by him and left. Finally, he proved unable to do even basic research or grasp a political point. After a series of clumsy errors, knowing how exasperated I was, he resigned before I could sack him. It was an acrimonious departure and he immediately started work for another UKIP MEP.

I became non-inscrit in the New Year. Around the time of the General Election in May 2010, my team and I found that documents, including itemised phone bills, were missing from the Birmingham office. I was very uncomfortable about this. I have some well known friends – household names. I'd had meetings with senior politicians who for a variety of reasons would not want it to be known that I was talking to them. Records of these discussions were confidential.

I could not be sure exactly when these documents had disappeared. But this was paperwork that Faustus had worked on and it did occur to me that he could have taken it when he left, or later, since my office had still been in the UKIP building after he'd gone to work for someone else. I reported the theft to the police at the time, but was told that there was insufficient evidence to press charges. It is an odd area of law; some of the missing data had been on the computer (and electronic information doesn't come under the Theft Act) but there were also physical records, such as telephone bills.

Then I discovered that yet more documents had gone. The police agreed that there was circumstantial evidence, but not enough to arrest Faustus. By this time some of the data was being put up on the internet – stuff that had been stolen as hard copy, including the employment contract of his successor.

August, 2010, was my first opportunity to take stock. It had been a tumultuous first year in office, with a lot of Human Rights work, a new office to set up, and mobile surgeries to organise. There had been many weeks of sixteen-hour days. But now, just as we were about to start our important referendum campaign, I did something I had not found time to do before. One of the things I'd learned in America was that you should occasionally sit at your employees' desks. So in August, 2010, this is what I did.

You take a look around the office. You see things in the way that they see things. It gives you a different perspective. Look at the screen in front of you. What are they working on? How do they do it? I noticed something slightly wrong about the expenses' claims in the system and when I got back to Brussels I told the relevant authorities. A lot of the data I needed to show them was among the material that had already been stolen, but I could see that my claims for travel to and from Brussels and/or Strasbourg didn't look right. It wasn't the dates or amounts so much as the method of travel. I drive a lot; putting the car on the Eurostar, you're across the Channel in half an hour. I do my best thinking when I drive. I come up with ideas.

I tried to find out when this had started to go wrong and asked the staff. It turned out to be a problem with the system that Faustus had put in place. He had been incompetent. I did not assume that what he'd done was deliberate; it was just riddled with errors, inaccuracies – it made me regret that I hadn't decide to sack him before he resigned.

I have, and never had, the remotest impulse to defraud the EU. Why would I? All you have to do to make money, legally, as an MEP is nothing. You could have your 'office' in the broom cupboard of your house, produce no magazines, newsletters or anything else. You could employ your spouse at whatever salary you deem appropriate. The current secretarial allowance is £215,000 a year and you can give it to one person. I use it to rent an office in Birmingham and employ a staff of eight.

As an MEP it seems you can claim a large salary, and many perks, yet do only as much, or as little, as you choose. Below is an excerpt from a newspaper article published in the Independent on 20 September, 2012, which is a scathing critique of UKIP's performance.

Between them, the party's 12 MEPs have tabled no reports, 11 have tabled no opinions, nine have signed no written declarations or motions, and seven have tabled no amendments to reports, ranking them at the bottom of the pile out of all 753 MEPs. Or at least that is what the Liberal Democrat MEP Chris Davies claims, after poring over the figures. "In Brussels the UKIP representatives reduce our country's reputation to that of a laughing stock. The nearest thing to a UKIP MEP you are likely to see is an empty seat," he said.

It could be argued that UKIP MEPs have better things to do than hang around in Brussels, since their mission is to get Britain out of the EU – an argument that would stand up better if they had not trousered £11.5 million in salaries, staffing and office costs. And that is not counting their expenses.

If I wanted to get rich the MEP's salary is an easy and legal way to do so. Instead I regularly break the EU working Hours directive by putting in 70 hours a week and £30,000 of my net salary is fed back into funding my work.

But the problem identified by my arrest was my signature at the bottom of claim forms from the late summer of 2009, my first couple of months as an MEP, when Faustus was responsible for my EU admin. Why had I signed these forms? Because I didn't read them. I had mountains of work, heaps of paperwork – and admin is what you employ staff to do. I was naïve enough to trust him.

Yet this police bail is a hell of a thing to have hanging over me. It may still be there next year when I stand again as an MEP. I have talked for hours about this with my solicitor, and decided to do nothing. I could spend around £30,000 to obtain a Judicial Review on the grounds that this is an unfair process, but if the judge declines to interfere with police work, as judges often do, then I'll attract headlines – 'MEP fails in her attempt to block fraud enquiry.' I could demand that the police either charge me or let me go; if they did decide to charge me, this too would mean headlines. Although it's likely that the case will eventually be dropped, mud sticks. It's axiomatic that there's no such thing as bad publicity. Of course there is.

That arrest in 2012 does not stop me from standing in the Euro-elections of 2014. But it is a big pebble to throw at me from the back of the crowd. I can only follow my solicitor's advice and carry on with my job. I am writing about it now only because it has to be acknowledged.

25 | BEING MYSELF

I consider myself incredibly fortunate. I have a job I enjoy, family I love and I have a special woman in my life, to whom I am deeply committed. She is a very private person and hates the limelight.

I live in a country that's relatively free; I can criticise the Government without fearing a knock on the door. I love my country. I am a patriot (definition: one who loves his or her country and supports its authority and interests). I appreciate what Britain is, and what it offers, all the more because I travel such a lot. Being British to me means having pride in a small country that's achieved more than most big ones. We have the right to stick up for what we stand for. History's shown that we don't give up and when faced with evil we put the interests of others above our own.

Being a euro-sceptic hasn't made me a little-Englander. I'm proud that we're inclusive and generous. We've always absorbed immigrants and have been the world's most successful melting pot since Roman times. In the seventies and eighties, the Union Jack was hijacked by far-right extremists and the whole idea of patriotism was polluted. Nationalism became a dirty word. But the 2012 Olympics reclaimed our flag, our national pride and our self-belief.

I was in the Olympic Stadium when British Somali-born runner Mo Farah won his *second* gold medal. The whole stadium adored him; eighty thousand of us screamed our enthusiasm and waved our Union Jacks and Mo celebrated by wrapping himself in the flag.

Britain is not perfect. I worry, for instance, that our religious freedom is being eroded by over zealous political correctness. If the Churches have no rights, the result will be conflict and isolation. And

I've struggled to accept our Government's immigration policies for the past thirty years – especially in the past decade.

One of my greatest passions has always been immersing myself in new and foreign countries and cultures and learning more about them.

My lasting memories of travel are of diversity – the thousands of people I've met and the way they live. Because of the nature of my work, I haven't always seen the bright side, but rather the results of political and economic systems that don't work and never will. I have seen desperate poverty in India, Africa and South America. I've seen how socialism failed in Cuba and how apartheid's legacy still scars the township of Langa outside Cape Town.

In 2010 I was the only UK MEP at Auschwitz for its annual commemoration of its liberation at the end of January, 1945. I wore seven layers of clothing and my teeth were chattering. The temperature was twenty below, exactly as it had been when the Red Army opened up the camp and found a few thousand starving, lice-ridden survivors in thin pyjamas, too sick to leave, half-dead with cold; and the gas chambers, capable of extinguishing 6,000 lives every day. A visit like that makes you work with renewed fervour for human rights everywhere.

My team and I are doing valuable work and need to carry on with it, but there are never enough hours in the day. I have friends I haven't seen since I was elected – occasionally we've exchanged a Facebook message, but otherwise, I simply haven't had time. I don't play sport anymore. I really miss playing football. I used to play for fun for a team affiliated to 'The Fox' a lesbian Bar in Birmingham. I struggle to find time to read for pleasure or go to the theatre as much as I used to, but I'm paid to put my constituents first.

Do I have a hinterland? Of course. When I desperately need to stop thinking about people trafficking, abuses of the Green Belt, or whatever work-related issue is my priority that week, I resort to football, 'Corrie', TV documentaries and the 1980s.

Football of course tops the list. I've got a hideously expensive Liverpool season ticket and frequently rant on 606, the phone-in programme on Radio 5 Live. I'm a Dons Trust member, so I see a lot of AFC Wimbledon's home matches in South London; and I go to West Midlands non-league matches and yell enthusiastically in support of our lot.

I have Coronation Street on auto-record. I've followed it avidly since I was a kid. I find brilliant documentaries on BBC Four. And I am a collector of genuine eighties memorabilia, which takes up an entire room in my home. The spare room in my house is the Fantasy Bedroom – the one I wanted when I was about thirteen – with Adam Ant posters on the wall, a Rubik cube, a Marathon bar, a Sinclair Spectrum computer, a bottle of Coca-Cola (labelled in commemoration of the Royal Wedding), and of course a record player, for my 80s vinyl.

I rent a small apartment in Brussels, but spend a lot of time travelling and staying in hotels. When I can't face another line in a 400-page report, I fish around in the bedside cabinet for the Gideon Bible, in English, which is usually there, offering comfort. I hardly ever go to Mass, but still count myself a Catholic, and if I'm in a strange city or near a church at home with time to spare I will go in and light a candle to St Anthony, my mum's favourite saint. I'm excited by Pope Francis, who's at the very beginning of his papacy and who I think will lay the foundations for reform. I'm encouraged by his recent reminder that the Church must show balance, and heal wounds, and his warning that it could fall 'like a house of cards' unless it changes. His Holiness has said that the Church preaches rather too often about abortion and gay people and needs to show greater mercy.

In rare moments of quiet reflection I think back on my life and how secure I feel now. I remember the tearful sixteen-year-old I was; travelling hopelessly back to Thamesmead after seeing the GP whose brutal words 'you'll grow out of it' had made everything go dark. I could see no future for myself. But somehow the years of pain and depression I went through after that have inspired an inner strength.

I now believe that I can succeed no matter how improbable it seems. And I can succeed in Britain, because we're the most tolerant of all the developed nations. Before publishing this book, I decided to commission a YouGov Poll on whether British voters would change their minds if they discovered that a candidate had had a sex-change. Two-thirds of people said it would make no difference and only ten per cent said they would be 'much less likely' to vote for the candidate.*

I'm often asked why I don't campaign for gay rights and haven't been a role-model activist. But while I'm deeply grateful to the many whose efforts have won reform in the law, and benefited from their commitment and perseverance, I've chosen a different route through politics. I'm now as legally female as any woman born. I feel passionately about all injustice or discrimination: true equality happens only when your colour, creed, gender or sexuality is not a label used next to your name. And we are not quite there yet.

*Please see appendix.

POSTSCRIPT | THE NEXT STEP

We in Britain don't have a fully participatory democracy. We're apathetic about a lot of issues because we're too ill-informed to understand them. The EU is one of those issues and it is far too important to ignore.

Week after week I speak to people who are sick of arguing about Europe. We have been in this terrible half-way house for nearly thirty years; neither fully committed players, nor outside the EU and in control of our own destiny. We need an informed public debate on our EU membership, which is both complex and problematic. In a democracy, misinformed public opinion is dangerous.

I recently spoke at a conference on 'The Phenomenon of Euro-Scepticism' at Leeds University. I said if people didn't like euro-scepticism, then they needed to face up to the euro-sceptics and have a national debate and a referendum. This was received with shock. Ordinary people couldn't understand the EU, said the academics present. I found that stomach-churningly arrogant.

On the other hand, if they're right, whose fault is it?

Where are 'ordinary people' supposed to find political information? Answer: the media and political Parties.

The media bears some of the responsibility for public apathy. It too often trivialises and is biased. The BBC is supposed to give both sides of the argument, but too often prioritises the views of the Confederation of British Industry. The CBI is pro-EU, just as it was pro-euro – demanding that we dump the pound.

As for relying on politicians for information – my background would indicate allegiance to the Labour Party. But the Labour Party sees the workers as forever the workers, and aspiration is too often an alien concept. This is the Labour Party that presided over the nadir of state education in the seventies; the Party that ignored more than a million marchers opposed to the Iraq invasion; the Party that claims to be fraternal, but is in fact paternalistic: patronising people at the bottom, discouraging access to better information, to more knowledge, more money, or more power. Labour seems not to respect us.

I became a Conservative because Margaret Thatcher permitted people like me to aspire. She expected of us, the millions on housing estates – opinions, self-betterment, ambition, action.

But the Conservatives since her downfall have failed to conserve and protect the United Kingdom. They, and mostly they, have given away our sovereignty, piece-by-piece, to the EU. There was nothing in the 1970 Tory manifesto about signing up to the Common Market. How could a Party that believed in a nation-state make us all citizens of the EU without a mandate to do so? We can't trust the Conservatives on Europe.

Nor do I believe they can be trusted to give us an In/Out referendum. David Cameron mutters about 'renegotiating.' We cannot renegotiate powers without a new treaty, and because a new treaty requires the unanimous consent of all EU members, it would require at least one other referendum, in Ireland. I don't see smaller countries kissing their own aspirations goodbye for our benefit.

But the EU fails us with its parliamentary system; in foreign affairs; in its legislation; and by obfuscating the price we pay. We have seventy-three UK MEPs. They do not work together, or in any significant national bloc, to further our interests.

One problem is structural. There is no mandatory structure for communication between MEPs and MPs and their Parties. As things stand our Chancellor or Home Secretary or Prime Minister can go into a meeting totally disengaged from what the elected British MEPs are saying. MEPs and their parties often communicate inadequately with one another, never mind their constituents.

And too few MEPs give their constituents value for money, including the one-third of British MEPs who are euro-sceptic. Some, like Dan Hannan and Nigel Farage, have an 'only euro-sceptic in the village' mentality. Their grandstanding takes up time that could be usefully employed for the voters' benefit. Of the pro-Europeans, a few put in a hell of a lot of work – Jean Lambert, a Green MEP for London, is always there. Malcolm Harbour, a pro-EU Tory, does a fair amount. (He is looking to become a Commissioner.) I'm on the Women's Committee, and I think more MEPs should be promoting real investment in childcare, as in the Northern European countries, with more equal male and female maternity/paternity leave.

But I suspect that a lot of pro-Europeans fail to make the case for Europe because they don't really have one. Or maybe it's because of arrogance, laziness and fear of rejection by the public.

Most MEPs, across all the regions, produce very little literature and don't even hold surgeries. They get the same allowances as I do (I personally subsidise my work to the tune of £30,000 a year). Why don't they have mobile surgeries? Why are they not engaging with their employers, the electorate? I guess it's because the EU lets them, and so do you, the voters.

Secondly; foreign relations. The EU's relationship with non-EU countries is shambolic. The only time I leave my euro-scepticism at the door is when I work on the Human Rights Committee. I try to stand up for self-determination in places like Kashmir. Yet the EU is too often supine. For every trade-related reason imaginable it avoids confronting the Indian Government, which has a dubious record on human rights, execution in particular. Being an MEP has allowed me to visit prisoners of conscience in Bahrain and Palestinians in Gaza, and I went with a delegation from the EU to Tunisia shortly after the Revolution. Although I pay particular attention to the major issues of debt and housing, thousands of immigrant families are worried about loved ones left behind in war zones. And none of us was elected to put all our efforts into problems suffered by any one section of the electorate.

203

Thirdly; EU legislation. The CBI represents shareholders: everyone with a pension, then. You can't contribute to a pension unless you've got a job. Small businesses employ 46.8% of the UK workforce. Small businesses struggle under a deluge of red tape from Brussels – compounded by additional rules that Whitehall has imposed.

As to our national trade interests – where were the pro-Europe MEPs when I went to Chile with an EU delegation recently? I was the only British MEP there. Britain has a lot of trade in financial services with Chile and the EU is actively looking to damage it.

Why would you want to attack a member state, a wealth creator? But if the EU is our partner, then ours would seem to be an abusive relationship. We over-compensate by obeying the EU's laws and paying its fines. Are we, as a nation, co-dependent? I would say we are.

EU legislators look at situations in the worst member states – in business, human rights, animal rights, women's rights, environmental issues – at one end, and the very best states at the other, then decree a median value. This is how they so often come up with a mediocre trajectory for action. A French MEP recently told a group of us that more employment legislation means more employment! As if a cost burden would create jobs.

Fourthly; the EU is sneaky. Electors in the West Midlands are unhappy about the HS2 rail link. It's going to cost a fortune and cause environmental damage, yet they have never been fully consulted or listened to with respect. Behind all this is the Trans-European Transport Network (TEN-T), of which HS2 will be an integral part. Across the EU as a whole, from 2007-23, some €285 billion of taxpayer's money has been allocated to it. This is never mentioned.

When renegotiation of our membership comes up, the attitude to a free trade agreement is defeatist. Why wouldn't we get one? We buy far more from the EU than we sell to them. They won't want us to turn our backs on their BMWs and Rioja in favour of Californian wine and Toyotas.

Then we're told we'll lose EU funding. What EU funding? The EU has no source of funds other than the member states. The UK is a net contributor, the second largest. Any money we get from the EU is our own, handed back by a third party whose accounts have failed to pass an audit for eighteen years.

To sum up: the EU, in my view, talks a lot more than it can act.

We should be making our own laws. In support of this I put forward: tax reform, and dispute resolution.

Our economic interests are being damaged by threatened EU taxes on financial transactions. We should be looking at reforming our own tax system. The EU is scared of our becoming a sort of EU Hong-Kong – an economic powerhouse. If London offered favourable tax rates without EU regulation (and the EU can't stop creating regulations – it can't help itself) this is what would happen, and all the other states know this. The City is already an elephant in a room full of cattle, where the European bourses are concerned. But the Lisbon strategy of 2005 was for the EU to be 'the most competitive and dynamic knowledge-based economy in the world, capable of sustainable economic growth with more and better jobs and greater social cohesion' by 2010. What happened?

As to individuals, wealth should be distributed more equitably, but in such a way that all parties want to create more wealth. If you unilaterally raise taxes on a single group of wealthy individuals they move to a state that isn't so greedy. Instead of getting only 10% of every hundred million, you get 100% of nothing.

We need a state-funded dispute resolution system to give businesses and employees confidence. American employment law hurts employees. EU regulations cripple small businesses. If you give employers confidence that they won't be bankrupted by court cases, and give workers confidence to use their initiative to find jobs, you have a successful economic engine. I don't see the EU, or for that matter our own Government, achieving this.

All opinion polls point to immigration as a major concern. The EU promotes free movement of goods, people and services among 500 million of us. Any EU citizen can live and work in any part of the EU. This would not necessarily be a problem if all member states were equal. But they're not. After 2004 and the inclusion of ten new member states, including those from the former Eastern Bloc, hundreds of thousands of people came to the UK looking for work. The Labour Government did not follow the more cunning French and Germans and put a two-year freeze on new member state workers. They underestimated the numbers who'd come, so public services such as education, health and housing were overwhelmed. The immigrants were hard-working people but they, rather than the politicians, unfortunately took the brunt of local hostility. Protest sounded (to Gordon Brown, notoriously) like bigotry. Yet Labour won't face its failure. Ed Milliband used the 2013 Labour Party Conference to talk about limiting non-EU immigration. That is not the problem. And nobody knows how many Romanians and Bulgarians will arrive after January 2014.

Negotiation should result in a win for both sides. For us, this means refusing to cave in to unreasonable demands because we've lost our nerve. We, who defeated the Germans and saved the French, somehow lack the backbone briefly supplied by Margaret Thatcher's leadership.

You may wonder why, if I am a Euro-sceptic, I am an MEP. Well, simply by publicising their cause and letting local constituents – like immigrant communities or military families – know that somebody cares. I have been a strong advocate for the missing people of Cyprus and critical of Turkey as it's tried to join the EU. I was visiting families in Cyprus last year when I learned the EU had been awarded the Nobel Peace Prize. I was on EU territory, part of which is illegally occupied by Turkey, and in Greece and Spain there were violent riots about enforced austerity. The Nobel Peace Prize?

I'm proud to do a huge amount of work on Kashmir, because the local community has asked me to. Kashmiris are fighting for self-determination. They were promised a referendum in 1948 by the UN and have still not had one, so their cause fits with mine.

I wanted to understand the concerns of military. 92% of British parliamentarians who voted for war in Iraq had no military experience. That kind of ignorance is not something to be proud of. So when I was invited to join the Armed Forces Parliamentary Scheme I did. I did a training course with the Royal Air Force, and was given the honorary rank of Squadron Leader. Among other things, I learned survival skills – being dumped into the sea off Cornwall, first with colleagues, inflating a team raft, and then doing the same again by myself and being hauled out of the waves by a Sea-King helicopter. The culmination of the training course was at Camp Bastion in Afghanistan: an assault landing in pitch black wearing body armour, strapped to the side of a C17 military aircraft. Business class it isn't.

The highlight of the visit was talking to the service men and women who do so much to protect our country. They worry about families at home. My team constantly pushes councils to look after service personnel and their families during and after service.

Another advantage of being an MEP is that I can agitate for us to leave the EU. I have learned, as a politician, how to mobilise an electorate. And I feel a duty to those 200,000 plus petition-signers to stand up for their beliefs at next year's European Election with the 'WE DEMAND A REFERENDUM NOW' campaign on whether to stay in the EU or leave it.

And suppose we, the Euro-sceptics, won a referendum, and the Government acted upon it?

How would we leave? UKIP, predictably, has failed to put together a manifesto blueprint that answers this question.

The truth is: with difficulty.

We have already allowed our legal system to be subsumed into the EU system. The Consolidation Acts alone would take at least two years of Parliamentary time. You can't just repeal the '72 Communities Act. Having enacted Article 50 of the Lisbon Treaty, which is the process for leaving, we would have to renegotiate a lot of laws and agreements. This means two years of negotiation in which our Parliament would set up Consolidation Acts to close loopholes in the law. We would also have to look at Free Trade Agreements, the first one being with the EU itself.

So getting out would take a minimum of two years, and a lot of work, and our legislature and executive could make the changes that quickly only if they postponed work on absolutely everything else. The EU is complex. But it is every politician's job to explain the case for and against.

We cannot have a national debate on EU membership if the electorate remains uninformed and we certainly can't have a truly democratic outcome to a Referendum.

So how can the electorate get the facts?

We need a special consultation process. The EU is like a marriage – the key to our future. I think we need a panel of people who are largely unconvinced one way or another, who will:

- Listen dispassionately to all the arguments from experts in different fields.

- Produce a brief, clear, report for distribution throughout the UK within one year of commencement.

- Put the case for and against in a succinct manner.

In the New Year we will be publishing our blueprint for a referendum and how we believe the public should be supplied with the facts, For and Against. There is more about the Panel in my election literature and at the end of this book.

As to the referendum, it must be fair and binding.

There have been unfair referenda before. Only a big carrot has reliably achieved a Yes vote for the European Union. Cyprus, Portugal,

Ireland, and Italy entered on the promise of huge infrastructural upgrades. Just about every old Irish voter was against the EU on abortion and divorce, but they still voted yes, and in flooded the EU money – that is, it flooded in to match, euro for euro, whatever their own Government put in, plus interest at preferential rates according to German credit ratings.

I assisted in the Irish referendum, and before that in the Danish one in 2000. The Danish Referendum took place during a particularly cold snap and the pro-EU campaigners were handing out warm coats to children. The vote went against them anyway – but it does seem that we need a cap on incentives. If a Kenyan politician had stood on a street corner offering free clothes to electors, EU observers would have said he was buying his votes. That's what 'fair' means.

As to 'binding' – if the people decide that we should stay in the EU, then the implicit message is that we must trust our MPs and our MEPs to negotiate in Britain's best interests. I do not think that we can do this from within the EU.

However, here we are: WE DEMAND A REFERENDUM NOW – not in 2017.

When Nigel Farage heard that, having presented the petition to the Government, I was still collecting to get the number of signatures up to 200,000, he invited me to tea at the Goring Hotel and tried to get me back into UKIP. No. UKIP cannot be trusted to take euro-scepticism to its logical conclusion. I also don't think for a minute he would want me back in the Party. What he really wanted was the database with more than 200,000 names and addresses of those who had signed the petition. And although he invited me to tea – and it was a very amicable meeting – he dashed out to take a call on his mobile phone and left me to pay the bill.

I am standing for the EU Parliament in 2014 because I have made it clear that I can be trusted. I've also made it clear that I am campaigning to achieve redundancy for all MEPs, myself included.

If my efforts succeed, I hope I will be elected to the British Parliament one day. If I don't get re-elected, I will nonetheless feel that I have done everything I possibly can for my constituents. No regrets, therefore. I'll know I did my best, with the same words always ringing in my ears. 'Never give up!'

© Nikki Sinclaire 2013

YouGov Survey Results

Sample Size: 1956 GB Results
Fieldwork: 19th - 20th September 2013

	Total	Voting intention				2010 Vote			Gender		Age				Social grade		Region				
		Con	Lab	Lib Dem	UKIP	Con	Lab	Lib Dem	Male	Female	18-24	25-39	40-59	60+	ABC1	C2DE	London	Rest of South	Midlands / Wales	North	Scotland
Weighted Sample	1956	X	X	X	X	598	488	409	949	1007	233	495	669	559	1115	841	250	636	419	481	170
Unweighted Sample	1956	470	565	150	220	609	487	443	930	1026	165	450	746	586	1345	611	276	645	372	498	165
	%	%	%	%	%	%	%	%	%	%	%	%	%	%	%	%	%	%	%	%	%

How important or unimportant is a political candidate's personal life and sexual orientation when it comes to deciding who you will vote for?

	Total	Con	Lab	Lib Dem	UKIP	Con	Lab	Lib Dem	Male	Female	18-24	25-39	40-59	60+	ABC1	C2DE	London	Rest of South	Midlands / Wales	North	Scotland
Very important	7	6	7	6	14	7	8	5	10	5	7	7	6	9	7	7	8	6	8	8	8
Fairly important	21	24	22	16	32	29	20	15	22	20	17	12	21	31	21	21	18	24	24	16	19
TOTAL IMPORTANT	28	30	29	22	46	36	28	20	32	25	24	19	27	40	28	28	26	30	32	24	27
Fairly unimportant	34	38	36	34	33	35	34	38	33	36	29	33	33	39	37	32	35	33	34	37	34
Very unimportant	31	28	31	41	19	26	31	39	32	31	43	39	34	17	32	31	33	30	29	32	35
TOTAL UNIMPORTANT	65	66	67	75	52	61	65	77	65	67	72	72	67	56	69	63	68	63	63	69	69
Don't know	6	4	4	3	2	3	7	2	4	8	5	9	7	4	4	9	6	6	5	7	5

Suppose that you learnt the candidate you were planning on voting for at the next election had had a sex change, would you be more or less likely to vote for them or would it make no difference?

	Total	Con	Lab	Lib Dem	UKIP	Con	Lab	Lib Dem	Male	Female	18-24	25-39	40-59	60+	ABC1	C2DE	London	Rest of South	Midlands / Wales	North	Scotland
I would be much more likely to vote for them	1	1	2	3	1	1	1	1	2	1	4	2	1	0	2	1	3	0	1	2	3
I would be slightly more likely to vote for them	2	2	3	4	0	2	1	3	2	2	5	2	2	2	2	2	1	3	1	2	3
TOTAL MORE LIKELY	3	3	5	7	1	3	2	4	4	3	9	4	3	2	3	4	4	3	2	4	5
It would make no difference and I would still vote for them	66	60	70	74	60	58	69	77	63	68	65	69	67	61	68	63	66	64	70	64	66
I would be slightly less likely to vote for them	14	21	13	8	18	22	12	9	14	14	13	9	13	20	14	14	13	13	16	14	14
I would be much less likely to vote for them	10	11	7	4	18	13	9	5	15	5	10	10	10	12	10	11	9	12	7	11	9
TOTAL LESS LIKELY	24	32	20	12	36	35	21	14	29	19	23	17	23	32	24	25	22	25	23	25	23
Don't know	7	5	4	6	3	5	7	4	4	9	4	10	7	5	6	8	7	8	5	7	7

ACKNOWLEDGMENTS

Writing this book turned out to be a far harder task than I envisaged. The hardest part was not finding what to say, but how to cut it all down to a manageable size. Literally tens of thousands of words were edited out. I take full responsibility for the contents of this book.

There are lots of people to thank, first and foremost my parents and family for their support. My wonderful staff in the West Midlands and Brussels who through their professionalism allowed me to take time out to work on this without it showing!

Hannah for helping me to get kick-started. Jo Knowsley for editing. David Perry for cover design. Roy Smiljanic for photography. Ian Taylor for typesetting. YouGov for polling services. Sarah Jones & Claire Furber for their administrative assistance.

A special mention and thanks to Nicole Carroll who spent hours of her free time, without which this book would not have made it, and to Josh O'Nyons and Gary Cartwright for their advice.

Thanks also to David, Daniel and Greg whose advice has been invaluable

Finally to Victoria and Catherine for your special insights and assistance.